The Power of Family-School Partnering (FSP)

■ ■ ■ ■ ■ ■ ■ ■ ■ ■ ■ ■ ■ ■ ■

A Practical Guide for School Mental Health Professionals and Educators

Cathy Lines ■ Gloria Miller ■ Amanda Arthur-Stanley

Routledge
Taylor & Francis Group
New York   London

Routledge
Taylor & Francis Group
270 Madison Avenue
New York, NY 10016

Routledge
Taylor & Francis Group
27 Church Road
Hove, East Sussex BN3 2FA

Printed in the United States of America on acid-free paper
10 9 8 7 6 5 4 3 2 1

International Standard Book Number: 978-0-415-80147-8 (Hardback) 978-0-415-80148-5 (Paperback)

Library of Congress Cataloging-in-Publication Data

Lines, Cathy.
    The power of family-school partnering (FSP): a practical guide for school mental health professionals and educators / Cathy Lines, Gloria Miller, Amanda Arthur Stanley.
        p. cm.
    Includes bibliographical references and index.
    ISBN 978-0-415-80147-8 (hardcover : alk. paper) -- ISBN 978-0-415-80148-5 (pbk. : alk. paper)
    1. Educational counseling--Study and teaching. 2. School children--Mental health services. 3. School psychology. I. Miller, Gloria Bley. II. Arthur Stanley, Amanda . III. Title.

LB1027.5.L485 2010
371.19'2--dc22   2010015910

Visit the Taylor & Francis Web site at
http://www.taylorandfrancis.com

and the Routledge Web site at
http://www.routledgementalhealth.com

Contents

List of Figures

List of Tables

Series Editors' Foreword

The *School-Based Practice in Action* series grew out of the coming together of our passion and commitment to the field of education and the needs of children and schools in today's world. We entered the process of developing and editing this series at two different points in our careers, though both in phases of transition – one (RWC) moving from the opening act to the main scene and the other (RBM) from the main scene to the final act. Despite one of us entering the peak of action and the other leaving it, we both continue to face the same challenges in and visions for education and serving children and families.

Significant transformations to the educational system, through legislation such as the *No Child Left Behind Act* and the reauthorization of *Individual with Disabilities Education Act* (IDEA 2004), have had broad sweeping changes for the practitioners in the educational setting, and these changes will likely continue. It is imperative that as school-based practitioners we maintain a strong knowledge base and adjust our service delivery. To accomplish this, there is a need to understand theory and research, though it is critical that we have resources to move our empirical knowledge into the process of practice implementation. For this reason, it is our goal that the books included in the *School-Based Practice in Action* series truly offer resources for readers to put directly "into action."

To accomplish this, each book in the series will offer information in a practice-friendly manner and will have a companion CD with reproducible and usable materials. Within the text, readers will find a specific icon 💿 that will cue them to documents available on the accompanying CD. These resources are designed to have a direct impact on transitioning research and knowledge into the day-to-day functions of school-based practitioners. We recognize that the implementation of programs and the changing of roles come with challenges and barriers and, as such, these may take on various forms depending on the context of the situation and the voice of the practitioner. To that end, the books of the *School-Based Practice in Action* series may be used in their entirety and present form for a number of practitioners; however, for others, these books will help them find new ways to move toward effective action and new possibilities. No matter which style fits your practice, we hope that these books will influence your work and professional growth.

The idea of family-school collaboration is not new to the fields of education and school psychology. There are a number of excellent resources that have been published on this topic, including the seminal text by Susan Sheridan and Thomas Kratochwill (2008), *Conjoint Behavioral Consultation: Promoting Family-School Connections and Interventions*. However, as with other areas included in our series, we identified a need for a practical guide to expand the traditional ideas and to further the practice of family-school collaboration.

It was a pleasure to work with Dr. Cathy Lines, Dr. Gloria Miller, and Dr. Amanda Arthur-Stanley, who provided us with a complete, yet concise guidebook that goes beyond the one-way model of building family-school relationships. In *The Power of Family-School Partnering (FSP): A Practical Guide for School Mental Health Professionals and Educators*, Lines, Miller, and Arthur-Stanley offer a multi-tiered model that is collaborative in nature. Through the steps outlined by these authors, parents and families are empowered to join with schools in the education of their children and to become an integral partner in the educational process. We believe this book highlights the heightened need for effective family-school partnering as an essential educational component and a cherished facet of everyday schooling.

The continued growth and expansion of the *School-Based Practice in Action* series would not be possible without our relationship with Mr. Dana Bliss and Routledge Publishing, who, from the start, have supported our vision and have trusted our judgment on topics and manuscripts to be included in this series. We are grateful for their belief in our idea of having a book series focusing on "action" resources dedicated to enriching practice and service delivery within school settings. Their dedication and belief in meeting the needs of school-based practitioners made the *School-Based Practice in Action* series a reality and a resource we are truly proud to be a part of. We hope that you enjoy reading and implementing the materials in this book and the rest of the series as much as we have enjoyed working with the authors on developing these resources.

Rosemary B. Mennuti, EdD, NCSP
Ray W. Christner, PsyD, NCSP

Series Editors, School-Based Practice in Action Series

Preface

We targeted several groups of professionals in writing this material. School mental health professionals can be prime candidates to help support family-school partnering. School psychologists, social workers, and counselors usually have training in families, systems, data use, and consultation/facilitation, although the extent and specificity may vary. In addition, school mental health professionals tend to serve the entire school in their work and do not usually have daily classroom duties, thus allowing them some flexibility in prioritizing time and responsibilities. This book draws primarily from the school psychology field but strives to link the ethical and professional concepts to school counseling and social work.

School administrators are the leaders in inviting families and staff to partner with each other. They are the ones who can allow shared committees and decision making, flexible hours, student focus, and data use in everyday practices. They "set the tone" and provide permission for stakeholders to shift their practices to include families. Classroom teachers and instructional specialists are the school staff members who work on a daily basis with students. By knowing and understanding family-school partnering practices, they can expand and enrich their teaching, helping families to support student school success at home. Higher education instructors can use this book in preparing professionals to work with families, integrating partnering into content and skill areas such as teaching reading, providing small group counseling, and learning classroom management techniques.

In addition to those in the education field, families and community resources might be interested in the materials in this book as they partner with schools in working toward student success. Specifically, it is helpful to have a shared framework, language, and expectations in a family-school partnering initiative. We designed the concepts and materials presented in this book to be jointly utilized by families and educators as they work together in sharing partnering responsibilities. Transparency and mutual acceptability to various partnering parties were intentional.

Acknowledgments

We gratefully acknowledge our families who so patiently supported this project: Jim, James, and Sean O'Brien; Joe and Erica Czajka; Michael and Henry Stanley.

We offer a special thanks to Michael Stanley, who provided his expertise in editing this work, and to Brook Bowers, who designed our logo, which we felt so aptly captured the heart of our endeavor.

We appreciate the visionaries at the Exceptional Student Leadership Unit of the Colorado Department of Education; they have included family-school partnering as one of the key components of the response-to-intervention (RtI) framework. We offer special thanks to Ed Steinberg, Daphne Pereles, and Cindy Dascher, who are leading this initiative.

The Cherry Creek School District in Colorado includes numerous professionals and families who contributed their expertise to this book. Mary Dove, Jim Harris, Suzette Calvillo, Mark Semmler, Paul Zimmerman, Meadow Point Elementary School Positive Behavior Support Team, and the Cherry Creek Special Education Advisory Committee all lent their knowledge and materials. Two social worker colleagues, Cam Short-Camilli and Gail Ploen, provided important ideas about the concepts and format.

We are grateful for the administration, teachers, staff, board members, and families at the Pioneer Charter School, who during the last several years partnered with us to forge a new path that furthered our understanding of the critical issues faced by dedicated individuals as they journey toward a new family-school partnering (FSP) vision.

We so appreciate the many graduate students who provided invaluable feedback over the last three years as we developed a new course designed to instill knowledge and passion for FSP in the next generation of school and community mental health providers. A special thanks is offered to the University of Denver *Family-School Partnering and Consultation* class graduate students (2010, spring quarter), who piloted this book as their text and continuously offered insightful and important feedback.

We thank the *School-Based Practice in Action Series* editors, Drs. Rosemary Mennuti and Ray Christner, for asking us to write a book about our passion, using our knowledge as practitioners.

Finally, we cannot express enough the gratitude we feel toward all those who have shared their stories with us over the past years. We hope our work honors their thinking and beliefs in the importance of FSP.

Introduction

Family and school as partners is a philosophy and way of thinking about forming connections among families and schools to foster positive school learning experiences for children and youth.

Christenson and Sheridan, 2001

Authentic, meaningful family-school partnering (FSP) is essential to ensure school success for children in the 21st century. Neither schools nor families can do it alone. Our society cannot afford to have students fail to complete their educations. Indeed, the time has come to promote strategic, sustainable FSP as a key component of every educational community, with the same status as curriculum, instruction, and classroom management. More than 30 years of research have shown that such practices have a large and positive impact on students' academic and social-emotional-behavioral success (Henderson & Mapp, 2002). The current federal education laws are clear in their mandates for families to be full and equal participants in their children's education. There are numerous governmental resources and a wealth of guiding literature supporting the partnering of families and schools.

With such strong research, resources, and legal support, however, it is a "puzzlement" (Nevin, 2008) why there continues to be mostly separate and sporadic partnering efforts in schools despite positive intentions on both sides. Most initiatives are traditional, volunteering-at-school experiences instead of evidence-based practices of families supporting learning in the home and school. Experts in the field cite the substantial barriers that are reported by both families and educators as a reason for this research-practice gap. Those most commonly mentioned challenges are lack of time, understanding, and role expectations. We attempt to reframe these barriers as "hurdles" (Ellis & Hughes, 2002) that can be navigated by simple strategic planning, using existing infrastructures, and reallocating resources. We feel that partnering cannot be another program, team, or add-on to already-full agendas. It must be linked to everyday practices supporting students' learning. Our goal is to offer guidance in planning, implementing, evaluating, and sustaining coordinated FSP through a tiered, data-driven framework focusing on student school success. We hope to offer a simple road map for educators and families.

FOCUS

In developing the content and tools for this book, we provide practical information that can be easily applied to the everyday practices of educators and families. As a result, there is a purposeful narrowness. We present summaries of the literature that support FSP and school reform versus extensive discussion of the topics and refer readers to specific resources that can be pursued for further information as needed. Similarly, federal laws and public policy work are briefly addressed, with other information sources cited. The importance of partnering with community resources is integrated throughout the book, but because this area is broad-based with a literature of its own, separate treatment is not provided.

Based on our experiences in the FSP arena, we decided that simple, "doable" partnering actions needed to be illustrated with sample forms, training materials, and data collection tools so that readers can efficiently implement FSP in a timely fashion. Because school staff and families tend to be on a continuum of partnering beliefs and practices, the tools in this book were developed to serve as a buffet of sorts so that consumers can choose and adapt those that fit the identified needs of their system. FSP should be efficient, simple, "living-and-breathing" actions as opposed to filed-away plans in formal documents.

We believe that FSP must be a "nonnegotiable" educational component, preschool through high school. There must be a pervasive "no excuses" attitude. It must become an automatic behavior exhibited by students, staff, and families across all school structures and activities. Because most schools have variable funding sources and current economic stresses, partnering work must be cost efficient, self-sustaining, and value added. This implies practices that can be readily incorporated into daily school life.

FRAMEWORK

The foundation of FSP in this book was developed by drawing from various theoretical concepts and research findings. Our framework consists of a shared philosophy that includes the importance of prioritizing student school success, establishing shared responsibility for education, and respecting differences in expertise and cultures, the culture of both the school and the home. Our definition is a simple one: *Family-school partnering is sharing responsibility for a student's school success.*

Student School Success

This book stresses that the prominent, pervasive reason for FSP is positive student outcomes. Students are the center of all partnering discussion and actions. Learning is coordinated between home and school. Students of all ages, cultures, socioeconomic levels, abilities, and behaviors can learn and succeed in school, but the supporting partnerships between families and school staff are needed to actualize that vision and more intensely for those who might struggle for any reason. A key aspect of this book is that all stakeholders need to clearly see and hear the commitment of a school to FSP "for the sake of the children." This helps adults overcome their hesitation and reallocate their time so that they can shift more comfortably into partnering behaviors.

Student school success is defined in measurable terms so that all partners can share in making data-driven decisions. Specifically, four indicators are identified for this book's purpose: (1) high school completion; (2) continuous academic progress; (3) engaged learning; and (4) prosocial/coping skills. Students are included in partnering discussions, actively linking home with school and monitoring their own learning. We also use the term *student* throughout the book, instead of *child* or *adolescent,* even when referring to families. This is to highlight the focus on school success and to allow representation across age levels.

Tiers and Data

We chose a tiered, data-driven framework with an ongoing, coordinated action-planning cycle to integrate FSP practices in this book. Several factors led to this decision. First, two widespread school reform initiatives are rooted in these working constructs, Response-to-intervention (RtI) (National Association of State Directors of Special Education, 2006) and positive behavioral interventions and supports (PBIS) (Sugai et al., 2005). Many school practitioners will have familiarity and comfort with these models. Also, fundamental elements of RtI and PBIS exemplify educational best practices: recognition of a continuum of needs in the population through tiers, the importance of prevention and effective "core curricula," data-based decision making, and evidence-based practices. The tiered structure allows allocation of appropriate resources based on need. Second, partnering sustainability is tied to integrating school-family actions into a shared stakeholder understanding so that there can be common language, measurement of success, and reinforcement of positive outcomes. Third, developing data mechanisms for measuring ongoing responsiveness creates momentum for continuous implementation. Finally, because families and school staff approach education from their own unique beliefs and perspectives, using objective data allows two-way communication, equal partnering, and efficient decision making around student success.

Acronym and Logo

Family-School Partnering (FSP) Logo

Acronyms lend validity and friendliness to concepts. Logos, or simple visual representations, can "brand" or consistently communicate a message. For these reasons, we developed the term, FSP, for family-school partnering and use it throughout the book. *Family* was chosen to be the first word in our term to stress the importance of the family partnering with the *school* in supporting education. We communicate our term through the logo that displays two figures, symbolizing a family and school, lifting a student upward, sharing in rising school success. We urge practitioners and family members to use both the term and the logo frequently as they were designed to be mutually acceptable in linking the two worlds of a student.

CHAPTERS, TERMS, TOOLS, AND RESOURCES

The book chapters are intended to be used flexibly in the interest of honoring the reader's needs and time. Each can stand alone, with specific content, tools, terms, and resources contained within the chapter. However, to conceptualize an integrated FSP framework, it is suggested that all material be reviewed initially to obtain a "goodness of fit" with the specific needs of a school. Chapter 1 defines FSP. There is graphic representation and description of the tiered, data-driven, FSP framework with student school success as the central focus. The legal and research rationale for partnering is explained. Chapter 2 provides theoretical, systemic, and cultural context for the philosophical partnering foundation. Universal, core processes, and practices for all students, families, and school staff are presented in Chapter 3. These processes and practices are adapted and grouped for families, students, and staff needing more targeted and intensive partnering opportunities as identified in Chapter 4. Data-driven planning for sustainable system change, using a simple action-planning cycle is described in Chapter 5, with descriptions of staff and family responsibilities. Existing and collected data sources are incorporated. In Chapter 6, lessons are applied from the field, and evidence-based programs are briefly reviewed to support "real-life" FSP. Identifying and navigating hurdles are important focuses so that stakeholders can visualize how partnering might actually work for them. An epilogue completes the book by describing a working FSP school and offering final FSP words.

Each chapter ends with key terms that provide a quick content reference and annotated resources so that readers can access more information as needed. Also, at the end of each chapter, we include specific tools that can be adapted for use by an individual or site. The tools, which were developed with educator and family input, are also available on the accompanying CD for electronic accessibility. Our intent is that a reader, after reviewing the book or a specific relevant chapter addressing his or her needs, will be able to confidently engage in FSP with students, families, and staff.

This book was written with the dream that we are truly at the "tipping point" (Gladwell, 2002) for students, families, and educators learning to partner for student success. Gladwell ended his book, *The Tipping Point,* with the following thoughts, and we echo them for the state of FSP:

> But if there is difficulty and volatility in the world of the Tipping Point, there is a large measure of hopefulness as well. Merely by manipulating the size of the group, we can dramatically improve its receptivity to new ideas. By tinkering with the presentation of information, we can significantly improve its stickiness. Simply by finding and reaching those few people who hold so much social power, we can shape the course of social epidemics. In the end, Tipping Points are a reaffirmation of the potential for change and the power of intelligent action. Look at the world around you. It may seem like an immovable, implacable place. It is not. With the slightest push—in just the right place—it can be tipped. (p. 259)

About the Authors

All three authors are passionate about the family-school part-nering topic and explicitly implement the practices described in this book in their varied settings. All authors have back-grounds in school psychology.

Cathy Lines worked with family-school partnering initia-tives in her previous role as mental health coordinator in the Cherry Creek School District. Currently, she is working with the Colorado Department of Education in developing and implementing the family-school partnering component of the state's RtI model. She teaches family-school courses to gradu-ate students and practicing educators. Cathy is the parent of two young adults, each of whom had unique family-school partnering needs during their years at home.

Gloria Miller is a full professor and current director of the Child, Family, and School Psychology graduate program at the University of Denver. She has integrated family-school partner-ing into all class requirements and developed, with her coau-thors, a specific course addressing this issue. She regularly consults with local schools working to enhance their vision of partnering with families. Gloria has been a principal or coprincipal investigator on numerous grants and professional development projects focused on integrating families into school-based prevention, transitioning, and the promotion of early literacy and social-emotional well-being. Both Cathy and Gloria were members of the Future of School Psychology Task Force on Family-School Partnerships. Finally, Gloria is most proud of the accomplishments of her daughter, a high school senior, who has provided many important life lessons about the rewards and challenges faced by parents who work full time and yet desire to stay meaningfully connected to their child's education.

Amanda Arthur-Stanley is a practicing school psychologist in the Cherry Creek School District. She works with families on a daily basis in her early childhood and child find settings. Amanda's recently completed doctoral dissertation focused on parent monitoring, maternal education, and adolescents' emotional closeness to adults. She is a parent educator in her district and provides staff development opportunities around family-school partnering. Amanda is a new parent to ten-month-old Henry.

The authors welcome questions and feedback on this book and its topic. Family-school partnering is an ongoing work. Please contact them.

Cathy Lines, PhD, NCSP
    Consultant
    clines1@comcast.net

Gloria Miller, PhD
    Professor, University of Denver
    Child, Family, and School Psychology
    glmiller@du.edu

Amanda Arthur-Stanley, PhD
    School Psychologist, Cherry Creek Schools
    aamandaarthur1@gmail.com

One

Framing Family-School Partnering (FSP)

Tell me I forget. Show me I remember. Involve me I understand.

Chinese Proverb

This chapter defines family-school partnering and its acronym, FSP, and presents a tiered FSP framework with a central focus on student school success. The legal and research rationale for such a framework is described.

After reviewing this chapter, the reader will

- Define FSP and the shift from traditional parent involvement
- Describe a tiered, data-driven FSP framework focused on student success
- Understand the legal and research rationale for FSP in relation to current school reform

Imagine every teacher, student, and family working together to create coordinated learning opportunities from preschool through 12th grade with the sole goal of promoting the success of all students. It is our passionate hope that such educational experiences will become the norm for the children of our nation. The vision for this book is built around FSP that can enhance students' school success in academic, social, emotional, and behavioral learning.

The term *family-school partnering* was selected to reflect several basic assumptions. *Family* emphasizes all primary caretakers, not only parents, who perform essential parental functions in a student's life and also includes the student. *School* refers to all school staff: administrators, teachers, specialists, office personnel, bus drivers, custodians, cafeteria employees, security officers, and support personnel. The term *partnering* is preferred over several other common descriptors such as involvement, engagement, participation, or collaboration because it (a) reflects intentional, bidirectional, equal positions; (b) emphasizes a shared focus on the individual success of each student by all participants; (c) underscores relationships and communication; and (d) is a verb, indicating ongoing, continuing interaction.

From these ideas, a simple definition emerged that guided the development of this book: *Family-school partnering is sharing responsibility for a student's school success.* We also coined a new acronym, *FSP*. Acronyms are useful for "branding" and endorsing an important concept. The FSP acronym also allows for more efficient communication about a multifaceted process. Thus, we hope that FSP, and its focus on jointly coordinated, home-school endeavors with mutual accountability for students' success, will be more fully integrated into existing educational practice.

A SHIFT TO FAMILY-SCHOOL PARTNERING

An important shift has occurred since the mid-1990s, that coincided with and contributed to the development of our FSP framework. The shift involves both terminology, which has moved from "parent involvement" toward "family partnering," as well as a shift in ideas about the role of families in education and the way that schools and families work together. The verb *partnering* is most reflective of this shift since it highlights a relationship involving close cooperation between parties having joint rights and responsibilities (Christenson & Sheridan, 2001). The shift in outlook greatly expands on previous parental involvement concepts by placing a greater emphasis on the need for families to share goals, contributions, and accountability with schools through access, voice, and ownership in informed decision making (Fantuzzo, Tighe, & Childs, 2000).

The ways that schools and families work together have shifted because of several factors, including an increased focus on accountability for positive student outcomes and research-based practices (Marzano, 2003) and the development of stronger family-school policies (Weiss & Stephen, 2010). This shift also can be attributed to the reauthorization of two major pieces of federal legislation, one focused on general education (i.e., No Child Left Behind [NCLB] of 2001) and the other on special education (Individuals With Disabilities Education Improvement Act [IDEA] of 2004). These newer federal policies have evolved to require greater family participation in schooling and in any educational decision about their student (i.e., NCLB and IDEA, respectively). While prior legislation emphasized the need for parental involvement, in too many cases this resulted in school-dominated, unidirectional models versus more inclusive, bidirectional models of FSP. Clear directives are now contained in each of these laws that require family members to be viewed as important contributors and equal partners throughout a child's education.

Thus, this shift, which has been at the forefront of many research, policy, and legislative and educational reforms, has been one of both beliefs and actions. Prior parent involvement models have been replaced by a stronger focus on FSP. This has moved us far beyond typical school-based involvement activities to efforts that require greater collaborative coordination between home and school to promote student learning. The result has been the generation of many new ways to engage families in their child's education, including innovative thinking about parent-teacher meetings and conferences, two-way communication between schools and homes, faculty and family training, homework assignments, and other routine educational activities. This shift also stresses the need for data-driven educational decision making, using objective measures to monitor progress over time. See Table 1.1 for a summary of these ideas.

OUR FSP FRAMEWORK

The framework adopted for this book is based on a strong desire to craft a common FSP vision. We created a three-dimensional, multitier pyramid structure with an FSP logo at the center to enhance this understanding (see Figure 1.1). This visual presentation was selected to represent our FSP framework for several reasons. In recent years, similar multilevel schematics of community mental health service delivery have been forwarded (National Association of State Directors of Special Eduction, 2006). This framework also has been widely adopted as a part of current educational reforms that similarly portray mental health and other school-based services at three levels (Burns & Gibbons, 2008; NASDSE, 2006; Thomas & Grimes, 2008). Thus, we felt that this model would be familiar to many families and educators. However, we adapted and modified this familiar pyramid model in several important ways.

Table 1.1 Shift From Parent Involvement to Family-School Partnering (FSP)

Parent Involvement	Family-School Partnering
• *Parent* refers primarily to parents.	• *Family* refers to all caretakers and the student.
• *Involvement* refers to an objective, highly visible activity by one agent.	• *Partnering* refers to an ongoing, joint action among more than one agent.
• School is the typical site of involvement, usually with participants engaging in structured volunteering, such as fund-raisers and organized events.	• Home, school, and community settings are all partnering sites, with a focus on a broad array of opportunities to increase student learning and school success.
• Education is viewed primarily as the responsibility of the school, with families often playing a limited or unclear role in supporting student school success.	• Education is explicitly viewed as a shared responsibility between home and school, with families playing a critical role in supporting student school success.
• School-parent meetings and conferences tend to be formally initiated by the school, with a primary focus on information, program eligibility, and school-administered plans.	• Family-school meetings can be initiated by the school or family members, with a primary focus on student school success and joint planning; students are included whenever appropriate and possible; much discussion can occur outside formal meetings.
• Separate learning opportunities are planned for staff and families.	• Joint learning opportunities are often planned so that staff and families can learn together.
• Homework is often given with the expectation of independent completion and with consequences for failure to comply.	• Homework is given after families understand expectations, and if a student fails to comply, solutions are jointly developed between the school and family.
• Communication is often shared one way from the school to the home, mostly through formal written formats.	• Communication is often shared two ways, from school to home and from home to school, through various means.
• A few parents tend to participate at school-based events and on school committees.	• All families are given opportunities to participate and to gain information, even if from home.
• Family data collection is isolated and demographic in nature.	• Family data collection is ongoing and relates directly to home-school partnering for student school success.

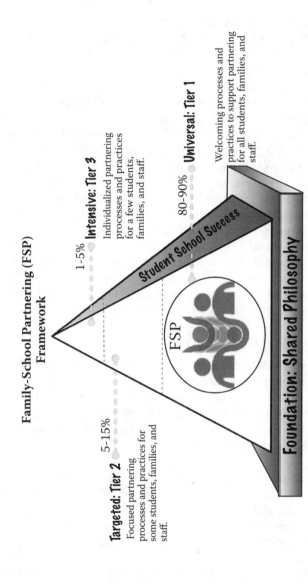

Figure 1.1   Family-School Partnering (FSP) Framework.

First, we added a base to the pyramid to reflect our belief that a core set of values is needed to provide a strong FSP foundation. The effectiveness and sustainability of FSP is enhanced when a shared philosophy is fully understood and accepted by all stakeholders. Second, this foundation supports three levels of FSP tiered processes and practices, at the universal, targeted, and intensive level, and broken lines between the tiers portray ongoing fluidity and a continuum of school, family, and community FSP services. This continuum of FSP services should depend on students', families', or teachers' needs or requests, which can shift or change over time. Third, we added another dimension to the pyramid to emphasize the interior "mortar" or structural "substance" that permeates all tiers. This third dimension reflects our belief that student school success is the "motivational glue" guiding all FSP efforts. Finally, at the center of the pyramid is an FSP logo. This logo displays two figures (i.e., families and schools) engaged in lifting a child upward. It was selected to underscore the parallel and relational nature of FSP with the goal of helping each and every student "rise to the top." The FSP logo was placed at the center of the pyramid to stress the interactive quality of data-driven FSP decisions.

Each of these concepts is further elaborated next and in greater detail throughout the remaining chapters.

AN FSP FOUNDATION

A strong FSP foundation provides basic philosophical values or tenets acceptable to all stakeholders. When FSP foundational beliefs are explicitly stated and simply framed, they combine with legal mandates and research findings to guide everyday practice. The following three foundational statements are the basis of our FSP philosophy.

1. Student school success is the center of FSP.
2. Education is a shared responsibility between home and school.
3. Families and educators each bring unique expertise and cultures.

These tenets must be understood and inherently adopted by all stakeholders. The first recognizes that a student and his or her success must be at the center of all FSP endeavors. The second acknowledges that joint educational efforts and relationships must occur between students, staff, and family members across school, home, and community settings. Finally, the third tenet of our FSP philosophy stresses the unique contribution and expertise of educators in regard to the culture of the school, and family members, in regard to the culture of the home. Cultural similarities and differences must be shared and honored so that student success is jointly supported by all participants from all perspectives.

FSP Tiered Processes and Practices

Our FSP framework is conceptualized as a continuum of three levels or tiers of processes and practices: universal for all, targeted for some, and intensive for a few. This model recognizes that families and educators may need different levels of partnering to support a student's school success. Boundaries between the tiers are permeable and fluid, which allows families and staff to obtain or request services across the tiers as circumstances change over time. *Tiered FSP processes* are regarded as essential interactions that can serve as a basic "to do checklist" of ingredients for successful partnering. *Tiered FSP practices* are regarded as the daily routines and activities in which educators and families engage to support children's academic and behavioral learning.

FSP processes at the universal tier are applicable to all students, families, and school staff and include building relationships, creating a welcoming setting, using two-way communication, and educating partners. These processes become the "cushion" that also supports targeted and intensive interventions. Partnering processes at the upper-level tiers (i.e., targeted and intensive) include all universal processes in addition to a fifth process called *teaming interventions*. This additional process focuses on the development of evidenced-based interventions, which can vary by degree of intensity, duration, or resource allocation. FSP teaming that occurs at the targeted and intensive tiers refers to shared efforts by family members, students, classroom teachers, school specialists, or community resources that occur if a student's learning or behavioral concerns at home or at school intensify.

In a tiered FSP framework, processes and practices differ based on resources and need. Within a tiered model, 80–90% of families, students, and staff typically benefit from universal FSP processes and shared practices. Focused partnering processes and practices with smaller groups may be needed at the targeted tier for some partners (i.e., between 5% and 15%). At the intensive tier, highly individualized partnering may be needed for a few students, families, and staff (i.e., 1–5%). Thus, in a classroom of 30 students, approximately 25 would flourish with universal FSP opportunities offered to all families and students, while another 1 to 5 students and their families might need more targeted or intensive FSP opportunities during the year.

Student School Success

The core substance of FSP that permeates and links all tiers is student school success. Student school success is a multidimensional concept best understood if explicitly formulated as measurable outcomes. Over the years, many indicators of student school success have been posed, including academic enablers (Christenson & Anderson, 2002), school engagement (Christenson, Reschly et al., 2008), and academic and social/emotional learning indicators (Christenson, 2004; Greenberg et al., 2003; Patrikakou, Weissberg, Manning & Walberg, 2003; Zins, Weissberg, Wang, & Walberg, 2004). The use of mutually understood and clearly defined indicators of student success is important for successful FSP. Objective indicators of student success create a common language and focused goal for all stakeholders. Such data can be used by teachers, students, and family members to formulate and monitor developmental progress. Students who understand specific success indicators are more likely to become informed partners in their own education (Epstein, 2001).

Throughout this book, student school success refers to high school completion as well as other widely accepted and understood indicators regarding continuous academic progress, engaged learning, and prosocial/coping skills. Specific and objective data sources for each of these student success indicators can be developed for groups and individuals that are applicable to all students, including those with disabilities, mental illness, or language differences. Examples of such indicators are listed in Table 1.2. Continuous academic progress is primarily measured by achievement test scores, benchmarks and progress monitoring, grades, and credit attainment. Engaged learning can be assessed through attendance, homework and classwork completion, and school event participation. Prosocial/coping skills can be addressed through student and teacher ratings, observation, extracurricular involvement, as well as reductions in office referrals, suspensions, and expulsions or danger/

Table 1.2　Student School Success Indicators and Possible Data Sources

Type of Indicator	Possible Data Sources
Continuous academic progress	Achievement test scores Benchmarks/progress monitoring Grades Credit attainment
Engaged learning	Attendance Homework completion Classwork completion School event participation
Prosocial/coping skills	Teacher/student ratings Observations Extracurricular involvement Office referrals, suspensions, and expulsions Threat/suicide risk assessments
High school completion	Graduation rates

suicide threat assessments. High school completion rates for individual students are typically tracked and linked to graduation criteria. While high school completion is the ultimate end goal, this long-term outcome is highly dependent on the successful attainment of many of the previously cited precursor indicators (Jimerson, Reschly, & Hess, 2008).

FSP Data-Driven Decisions

The importance of collecting and using data in an ongoing manner is crucial to the overall success of any FSP effort. Decisions regarding the implementation of specific FSP practices should be guided by data and consistently evaluated for effectiveness. Time and resources in education are too valuable to waste on efforts that are not effective. For these reasons, data-driven decisions are a key element of FSP.

Data-driven decisions occur when factual information (i.e., measurements or statistics) is used as a basis to identify and select specific actions (adapted from Merriam-Webster, 2004). A key aspect of FSP is that all parties are provided with the same facts and share in data analysis to reduce the tendency for decisions to be based on perceptions or past experiences (Raines, 2008). Data-based decisions are crucial so that FSP efforts can be strategically tailored based on objective indicators from existing as well as newly created sources. In a field with more descriptive than experimental or quasi-experimental research, there is a strong need to emphasize data-based decision making to inform current and future educational endeavors (Christenson & Carlson, 2005).

A systematic, data-based decision-making process similar to that applied within response-to-intervention teams is employed to guide the implementation of our FSP framework (Burns & Gibbons, 2008). A four-step action-planning process is recommended to define, plan, implement, and evaluate all FSP efforts. This four-step cycle is easy to understand and can be applied to partnering efforts by individuals, teams, committees, organizations, or entire schools. During the first two steps, data from multiple existing and newly created sources are collected, analyzed, and applied to planning. Specific goals, actions, and progress measures are implemented during Step 3 based on the data, cultural, and site relevance. These planned steps can avoid random acts of partnering often deemed ineffective or limited in scope. Finally, in Step 4, all FSP efforts are evaluated for effectiveness using student school success and other indicators to decide to continue or to develop a revised FSP plan. Each step of this FSP action-planning cycle is described in more detail in Chapter 5 in conjunction with specific FSP data collection tools.

THE RATIONALE FOR FSP

Successful implementation is enhanced when families and educators understand the rationale for the shift to FSP. Effective and sustainable shifts require "buy-in" and a reason to operate differently (Johns, Patrick, & Rutherford, 2008; Raines, 2008). It is important to provide a clear rationale that is not just based on opinion or expert recommendations. In regard to FSP, the legal and research evidence is strong and convincing. A brief overview of the legal precedents and research literature supporting FSP is presented next. A slide presentation for school staff and families, explaining this FSP rationale related to the framework, has been designed for adaptable site use.

 Check Out This FSP Tool: *FSP Legal and Research Rationale Stakeholder Slides*

Legal Precedents for FSP

For the first time in the history of our country, the two federal laws governing both general and special education were reauthorized and "positioned to work together." Both laws clearly mandated full parent participation in their child's education (Cortiella, 2006). In the reauthorization of the Elementary and Secondary Education Act passed in 2001, which guides general education policy in the United States (i.e., also known as No Child Left Behind, NCLB), there was a specific call for "local education agencies to assist school personnel to reach out to, communicate with, and work with parents as equal partners; implement and coordinate parent programs; and build ties between parents and the school" (NCLB, 2001, P.L. 107–111, 1118). This law also specified the need for scientifically based research in regard to instructional methods, accountability for all students' progress, strategies to enhance parent involvement, and for parents to have full access to information about school- and child-related performance (Cortiella, 2006). A statutory definition of *parental involvement* was also included:

> the participation of parents in regular, two-way, and meaningful communication involving student academic learning and other school activities including assisting their child's learning; being actively involved in their child's education at school; serving as full partners in their child's education and being included, as appropriate, in decision-making and on advisory committees to assist in the education of their child. (NCLB Action Briefs, 2004, p. 2)

Other specifications about parent involvement were outlined in the title sections of this law that are relevant to most districts across the country (U.S. Department of Education, 2003). In particular, a written parent involvement policy or "compact," jointly developed by parents and school professionals, that highlights shared responsibility for academic achievement is required. Unfortunately, there are few provisions for enforcement of any of these parental involvement components (NCLB Action Briefs, 2004).

IDEA, reauthorized in 2004, guides educational policy for children with disabilities and includes an increased focus on parental involvement (Cortiella, 2006). This law was strongly influenced by the findings put forth by a publication of the

President's Commission on Excellence in Special Education (2002): A New Era: Revitalizing Special Education for Children and Their Families. In this report, there was a call for special education reform to reflect similar mandates required in the NCLB Act. The reauthorization of IDEA incorporated many of the ideas from this commission ensuring that high academic standards, accountability, enhanced teacher quality, and reforms based on scientifically rigorous research were included as well as language requiring the participation of families (Chapman, 2005). In this legislation, families were to be more explicitly included, as evidenced by the following statement:

> The education of children with disabilities can be made more effective by strengthening the role and responsibility of parents and ensuring that families of such children have meaningful opportunities to participate in the education of their children at school and at home. (IDEA, 2004, 20 U.S.C. 1401(c)(5)(B))

IDEA 2004 also strengthened the role of parents as full and equal members of multidisciplinary teams, making it clear how parents are to be involved and given explicit information when a child is referred for special education. Parents are to be included in all data analysis, decision making, and intervention planning for any special education eligibility decision, but particularly when determining eligibility for a specific learning disability (U.S. Department of Education, 2006). To implement this law, districts and schools have begun to institute major system changes (NASDSE 2006; Schmoker, 2006; Wellman & Lipton, 2004). Unfortunately, there is a growing consensus that neither NCLB nor IDEA has helped to significantly close the achievement gap or improved educational outcomes for all children (Weiss & Stephen, 2010). As a result, many individuals are now calling for even greater fundamental changes and resources to further initiate and sustain family-school and community partnerships (Fege, 2008).

Research Precedents for FSP

Federal mandates and regulatory guidelines have in part been fostered by the results of prior research that overwhelmingly supported the major role families play in promoting children's academic achievement and other social and emotional outcomes (U.S. Department of Education, Office of the Secretary, Office of Public Affairs, 2003). Clark (1990) was one of the first to point out that, in the United States, students spend over

90% of their waking hours from birth to age 18 outside school, and this percentage remains above 70% if calculated only for school-age students. This finding spurred much work on the role of families and learning outside school. For over 20 years, the Harvard Family Research Project has been generating and summarizing research highlighting the importance of such issues and the need to align learning systems, such as home, school, afterschool, and summer programs (Bouffard & Malone, 2007; Little, 2009). Other researchers have illustrated a multitude of positive outcomes associated with greater family involvement and partnering in education (Christenson, 2004). Due to space limitations, only selected findings from this extensive evidence base can be presented. Excellent summaries of this work can be found elsewhere (Christenson & Sheridan, 2001; Epstein et al., 2002).

In general, researchers have demonstrated positive outcomes: (a) For students, these have included higher achievement, homework completion, and school attendance and completion; (b) for families, these have included more confidence in knowing about school and how to help their child learn; and (c) for teachers and schools, these have included improved morale, higher ratings of teachers by parents, higher performance ratings of teachers by parents and administrators, and greater community support of school finance and bond issues (Christenson, 1995, 2004). Researchers also have demonstrated that generalization of school learning occurs more readily when there is collaboration among educators, families, and community members (Sheridan, 1997), and when students perceive school and home as sending similar messages, they are more likely to display greater achievement (Epstein et al., 2002). Indeed, family involvement in education over time has been found to be a more significant predictor of such outcomes than a range of other factors (Weiss & Stephen, 2010). Henderson and Mapp (2002) drew the following conclusions following an extensive research review: (a) Programs and interventions that engaged families in supporting their children's learning at home were linked to higher student achievement; (b) family involvement appears to have a protective effect on children as they progress through the educational system; and (c) the more families supported their children's learning and educational progress, the more their children tended to do well in school and to continue their education. Similar conclusions also have been drawn by other syntheses of this research (Christenson & Reschly, 2010; Epstein et al., 2002; Jeynes, 2007; Marzano, 2003; Simon, 2001).

However, it also is important to understand the parameters of the research supporting FSP. Much prior research has been descriptive or correlational in nature, which does not allow for causality determination (Henderson & Mapp, 2002). Methodological and reporting variations and the multidimensional measurement required to assess the effectiveness of family-school-community partnerships also make it difficult to compare results across studies (Mattingly, Prislin, McKenzie, Rodriguez, & Kayzar, 2002). Finally, the degree to which causal or indisputable conclusions can be made is hindered by the significant challenge of performing either quasi-experimental or experimental studies in education and with families in particular (Christenson & Carlson, 2005).

Nevertheless, since the mid-1990s, there has been consistent, convincing, and credible evidence pointing to the positive impact of FSP on almost every indicator of student school success based on numerous meta-analyses and literature reviews, case and correlation studies, as well as quasi- and experimental research (Jeynes, 2007). When schools, families, and community groups work together to support learning, children tend to do better in school, stay in school longer, and like school more (Henderson & Mapp, 2002). This view is best reflected in a summary statement by Henderson and Mapp (2002), who after an extensive review of the FSP literature, concluded that: "Taken as a whole, these studies found a positive and convincing relationship between family involvement and benefits for students, including academic achievement. This relationship holds across families of all economic, racial/ethnic, and educational backgrounds and for students at all ages" (p. 24). Such positive results also are more likely when school, family, and community partnership programs are well planned and carefully selected (Henderson, Mapp, Johnson, & Davies, 2007). Thus, most experts in the field agree that FSP is a key moderator and mediator of student school success.

Professional and Policy Implications for FSP

Continued research and leadership at all levels is crucial if there is to be a sustainable shift to FSP. To strengthen the evidence base on effective FSP, Raines (2008) has stressed that all professionals must become intervention researchers who appraise and evaluate any new initiative by collecting meaningful effectiveness data. These recommendations also have been echoed by national organizations that represent school-based mental health professionals (i.e., American School Counseling Association, 2004; National Association of School Psychologists, 2000, 2005; National Association of Social Workers, 1999, 2002) through ethical guidelines and professional standards of practice and by publishing major position statements and articles regarding the impact and need for effective FSP. One example is the work of the Future of School Psychology Task Force on Family-School Partnerships (2007); this group was created in 2002 following a national conference to work on two goals that were set for the field: to enhance family-school partnerships and parental involvement in schools and to increase families' ability to support students. The action steps to achieve these goals included identifying evidence-based practices, developing preservice and in-service training modules, and working to integrate family-school partnerships into educational practice. The resulting six modules that were developed from this work can be accessed at their Web site (http://fsp. unl.edu/).

Weiss and Stephen (2010) have called for ongoing, data-driven evaluation to be an essential component of any national or local FSP policy. These researchers identified five major barriers to and gave recommendations for how to improve FSP in the future: (a) create more coherent policies and resourced programs to overcome fragmentation and "siloed funding"; (b) increase capacity building and training to overcome limited or ineffective compliance with major FSP initiatives; (c) develop exemplary pre- and in-service training models about how to partner with families to overcome the limited preparation of educators and other professionals who work directly with families and communities; (d) provide funding to enrich complementary learning experiences outside school to overcome access inequities experienced by many children; and finally (e) advance methods that foster changes in attitudes and create a sense of shared responsibility to overcome common issues of power, control, and accountability in education that can hinder the adoption of effective FSP processes and practices. In most cases, this means that families and educators must recognize and overcome fears of inadequacy, potential conflict, and prior negative experiences and commit to ongoing efforts to increase knowledge and to develop expertise to build future FSP capacity and sustainability.

KEY TERMS

- **Data-driven decisions:** Always using various forms of data to plan and evaluate, both in planning FSP and in supporting student success through the tiers.
- **Family-school partnering:** Sharing responsibility for a student's school success.
- **Foundation:** The shared philosophy that focuses on joint responsibility for student school success, acceptance of explicit areas of partner expertise, and mutual sharing of the home and school cultures.
- **FSP:** The acronym for family-school partnering, allowing for shared communication among stakeholders, including school staff, students, and families.
- **Partnering:** A verb indicating ongoing relationships and strategic actions.
- **Practices:** Everyday educational activities and events at home and at school that reflect partnering processes.
- **Processes:** The core curriculum and essential ingredients of FSP: building relationships, creating welcoming settings, using two-way communication, educating partners, and teaming interventions.
- **Shift:** Significant shift in research and practice related to FSP; shift from unidirectional, parent involvement to reciprocal, ongoing partnering with families.
- **Student school success:** Four measurable indicators that define school success for all stakeholders: high school completion, continuous academic progress, engaged learning, and prosocial/coping skills.
- **Tiers:** Universal and upper tiers of partnering processes and practices so that all families and staff are successfully supporting student success with timely effectiveness.

TOOL DESCRIPTION

FSP Legal and Research Rationale Stakeholder Slides.
These slides can be adaptively used to share the FSP
rationale with families and staff; they offer ideas for
discussion and activities (CD only).

RESOURCES

Web Sites

*Future in School Psychology Task Force on
Parent-School Partnerships:* http://fsp.unl.edu/

Includes various training modules on family-school partnerships for graduate students, practitioners, or university
instructors. Also has specific practical modules for teachers
in how to support families of children with disabilities in academic and behavior learning.

Harvard Family Research Project: http://www.hfrp.org

Researches and compiles expert information on early education and care, out-of-school learning, and family and community involvement in education. Publishes newsletters and
research reports, houses databases, and offers resources to
practitioners, policy makers, and families.

*National Coalition for Parents in
Education:* http://www.ncpie.org

Serves as a source for legislative and policy information for
member organizations, which include many national professional and advocacy groups. Includes resources for families,
educators, and policy makers.

*SEDL National Center for Family and Community
Connections With Schools:* http://www.sedl.org/connections

Provides research-based information that can be used to effectively connect schools, families, and communities. Highlights
research that is directly linked to academic achievement and
overall school success.

UCLA Parent/Home Involvement in the Schools:
http://smhp.psych.ucla.edu/qf/homework.htm

Serves as resource for information on schools working with
families from a variety of sources. Is a component of a Web

site devoted to supporting learning in schools through policy change, removing barriers, and collaboration.

Books

Christenson, S. L., & Reschly, A. (2010). *Handbook of school-family partnerships.* New York: Routledge.

Summarizes the evidence supporting partnerships with families. Is a comprehensive review of the history, science, and future research and policy agenda of the school-family work.

Leuder, D. C. (2000). *Creating partnerships with parents: An educator's guide.* Lanham, MA: Scarecrow Press.

Includes practical ideas for school staff in working with parents within a model of "self-renewing" partnerships and 13 specific implementation steps.

Marzano, R. J. (2003). *What works in schools: Translating research into action.* Alexandria, VA: Association for Supervision and Curriculum Development.

Summarizes 35 years of education research that identifies the most important factors in student achievement. Includes home environment and parent involvement in schools.

Thomas, A., & Grimes, J. (2008). *Best practices in school psychology* V. Bethesda, MD: National Association of School Psychologists.

Highlights key family-school-related practices in numerous summaries and throughout articles addressing other school psychology interventions, including ethics and position statements.

Two

Building an FSP Foundation

Truth and trust grow out of a dynamic interaction in which
listening for truths is just as important as telling them.

Lawrence-Lightfoot, 2003

This chapter highlights the core family-school partnering
(FSP) philosophy. We draw from ecological systems theory
(Bronfenbrenner, 1979, 1986) as a foundation for the FSP frame-
work and philosophy and discuss the conceptual influences of
Epstein, Hoover-Dempsey and Sandler, and Christenson and
Sheridan, who have contributed the groundwork for a tiered
FSP model. We highlight the importance of acknowledging
and sharing culture throughout FSP.

After reviewing this chapter, the reader will

- Identify critical philosophical beliefs underlying a
  unified vision of FSP
- Identify the contributions of four major FSP conceptual strands
- Discuss the role of diverse family and school cultures
  in FSP

As noted in Chapter 1, there has been a significant shift in
thinking from the traditional model of unidirectional parent involvement to a more inclusive, expansive model of FSP.
While the original push for parent involvement in the schools
was positive, new ways of thinking about families and schools
have continued to evolve. Shifts in research and the law, including No Child Left Behind Act of 2001 and the Individuals With
Disabilities Education Improvement Act of 2004, have reflected
the changes and made clear directives for schools to consider
families throughout education. While traditional conceptions
of parent involvement typically reflected school-based actions
on the part of the parent (e.g., volunteering at school), newer
versions of parent involvement stress ongoing partnering,

two-way communication, and the coordination of the home and school for learning activities. Community agencies collaborate as partners when needed, and all family members, not only parents, are invited to partner. Families are offered the opportunity to be involved from the start, often in new and creative ways, and both staff and families are encouraged to collect data to get an accurate picture of the student. The shift from traditional parent involvement to FSP also involves a shift in vocabulary. It is often helpful for partners to have a common language focusing on shared beliefs and understandings. Families, educators, and community members can encourage each other to practice using a partnering vocabulary as they work together. The shift to FSP from parent involvement is one of both beliefs and actions.

Part of this transformation in thought and action is a compelling need for a strong philosophy. Philosophy, like a mission statement, expresses one's core beliefs and forms the foundation for the framework. Perhaps most important, philosophy forms the core belief system that will allow people to make significant changes in their behavior. While the earlier, traditional model embodied excellent ideas and intentions, it was piecemeal and did not offer a cohesive framework to capture the many facets of FSP. Therefore, we start with forming our philosophy as the foundation for the FSP framework. Most simply, in creating the FSP philosophy, we must pull from what we already know and from the ideas that brought us to where we are today. First, we discuss ecological systems theory for its signature influence on how we see families and school as operating within systems. Next, we describe three additional conceptual strands whose significant contributions to FSP have helped make the shift possible for families and schools. We also discuss the central role of culture, describe the unique cultures of the family and the school, and present ways to acknowledge and embrace cultural differences within FSP.

AN FSP PHILOSOPHY

Understanding the uniqueness of home and school is especially important in our vision of effective FSP and therefore has an impact on our FSP philosophy. In building our shared beliefs of FSP, we sought to create a philosophy that is simple, practical, and guiding for tiered partnering efforts across two substantial systems, the family and the school. The philosophy serves as the foundation from which all FSP beliefs and behaviors flow. Student school success continues to be at the forefront of our FSP belief system as it comprises the substance of FSP. We considered three overarching philosophical beliefs that underlie our FSP vision:

1. Student school success is the center of FSP.
2. Education is a shared responsibility between home and school.
3. Families and schools each bring unique expertise and cultures.

Student School Success Is the Center of Family-School Partnering

We envision the student as central to our model. The student always remains the center of the framework and therefore the partnering relationship. Furthermore, we focus FSP explicitly on student school success as the desired outcome based on the compelling evidence that family involvement in schooling has been linked to positive changes in student school achievement (Henderson & Mapp, 2002; Sheridan, 1997). As discussed in Chapter 1, student school success is a multidimensional concept, defined for purposes of the FSP framework by high school completion, continuous academic progress, engaged learning, and prosocial/coping skills. Students are included throughout FSP as informed, active, and engaged partners.

Education Is a Shared Responsibility Between Home and School

Education is described as a shared, joint responsibility between the home and the school. No longer home- or school-centric, both parties are responsible and invested in a student's school success. While there has been debate regarding whether families, in addition to schools, are responsible for their children's learning (de Carvahlo, 2001), we believe that all children must be given every opportunity to succeed in school. As research substantiated, when families and schools work together in the joint interest of the child, children fare better in school (Henderson & Mapp, 2002; Marzano, 2003).

Families and Schools Each Bring Unique Expertise and Cultures

Families and schools may be very similar or very different. Previous ideas suggested that aligning the home and the school can certainly support student school success (Epstein et al., 2002). Although alignment of the home and school can be powerful, it is not always straightforward or easy to achieve. In our FSP framework, we believe that families and schools each bring unique expertise and cultures, including aspirations, values, beliefs, traditions, and behaviors that can affect the student. Sharing their unique expertise and cultures sets the stage for optimal problem solving and allows for surprising and exciting avenues for partnering.

MAJOR INFLUENCES ON FSP PHILOSOPHY

Bronfenbrenner

Bronfenbrenner's ideas about human development were instrumental in our framework of FSP, both for his focus on interrelated systems and the centrality of the family and school in a student's development. Most important, Bronfenbrenner's ecological systems theory provides a model to organize and understand the interrelated systems that can have an impact on home and school settings and hinder or enable FSP efforts (Ysseldyke & Christenson, 2002). His model, originally proposed in 1979 and updated in 1986, has had a tremendous influence on FSP research because it captures the complexity of family-school relations (Weiss, Kreider, Lopez, & Chatman, 2005). A child's growth and development are hypothesized to be influenced by the reciprocal interplay of factors across the micro-, meso-, exo-, and macrosystems.

The *microsystem* refers to contexts with the most immediate impact on a child, typically the home and school, and includes individual attributes and interpersonal exchanges within these settings. The *mesosystem* refers to the quality and quantity of interpersonal interactions between and among the individuals in these settings, which is most directly tied to the continuity of connections between home and school. The *exosystem* refers to contexts that indirectly influence the child because of their impact on individuals or institutions that can influence interactions within and across the micro- and meso-systems, such as a supportive or obstructive workplace, neighborhood, church, or community agency policies and practices. For example, a parent who is expected to work overtime is constrained from helping with homework, or a community board's decision to stop offering transportation may make it more difficult for parents to meet with teachers at the school. The *macrosystem* refers to political, economic, and cultural influences that have an indirect impact on the condition and access to resources and other opportunities for a cohort of same-age peers. Included in the macrosystem are the laws referred to in Chapter 1 that mandate family involvement in special education, Title I, NCLB, and other federal initiatives.

It is important that the student is always at the center of Bronfenbrenner's model and that the home and school are viewed as the two most critical contextual determinants of development, with neighborhoods, communities, and the larger sociocultural and political context exerting important but more indirect influences. Framing FSP through a systems lens honors the importance of context and recognizes the interrelated and reciprocal relationships that exist among students, families, schools, and communities. Many researchers have substantiated Bronfenbrenner's major claims by documenting the importance of family and school factors that mediate and moderate a child's school success (Astone & McLanahan, 1991; Grolnick, Ryan, & Deci, 1991; Hoover-Dempsey & Sandler, 1995, 1997; Teachman & Paasch, 1998). Bronfenbrenner's ideas serve as the primary foundation for our FSP philosophy and have made a tremendous impact on the field of FSP.

Further Influences on FSP

Three additional FSP conceptual strands have been instrumental in promoting our understanding of data-driven, tiered FSP practice. While each strand is presented individually, many of the core FSP beliefs are interconnected and build on one another and on ecological systems theory. Due to space limitations, only a brief overview of each strand is provided; further references and associated resources are included at the end of the chapter.

Epstein

In a theoretical model, originally proposed by Epstein in 1987 and further elaborated in recent years (Epstein, 1995, 2001; Epstein, Coates, Salinas, Sanders, & Simon, 1997; Epstein et al., 2002), FSP is conceptualized as overlapping spheres of interpersonal relationships across school, family, and community environments. A major assumption is that children do best academically when there are collaboratively developed and shared goals (i.e., overlap) across the spheres. The more "overlap" between homes, schools, and communities, the greater likelihood the child will experience academic success (Simon & Epstein, 2001). This model also provides a typology that organizes partnership activities into six areas viewed as critical to the development of successful FSP. This typology has led researchers to further conceptualize and formulate specific research questions on the nature and effects of such partnerships and has helped educators and families to systematize their partnership activities and practices (Simon & Epstein, 2001).

The first area identified in this typography, titled *parenting*, focuses on activities that foster a climate of acceptance as well as on conditions that support children's learning and behavior at all age levels. The second group of activities focuses on *communicating* and highlights practices that enhance regular, meaningful, two-way communication from school to home and from home to school. The third area, *volunteering*, relates to involving families as volunteers and audiences at school through modifying work schedules and recruitment practices. The fourth area stresses *learning at home* and emphasizes practices that can support a family's ability to play an integral role in student learning, including meaningful curriculum-related home activities. The fifth area, *decision making*, describes developing parents as leaders and participants in school decisions. The sixth and final area covered by this typography is *collaborating with the community* to stress practices that involve the coordination of family and school-based community resources and services to enhance student learning. The National Parent Teacher Association (PTA) adapted this typography in their national standards in 1998 and recently updated and retitled these standards in 2009 (National PTA, 2009), specifying the standards as welcoming all families into the school community, communicating effectively, supporting student success, speaking up for every child, sharing power, and collaborating with the community.

Each of these involvement practices has been found to independently and collectively influence parents' motivation to become further engaged in their child's schooling over time and students' schooling outcomes (Epstein et al., 2002). The influence of these practices also depends on prior partnering experiences, the attitudes of teaching staff and family members, and the age of the student (Bridgeland, Dilulio, Streeter, & Mason, 2008). As listed in our Web resources, the national Center on School, Family, and Community Partnerships has been formed of school districts across the country that have used this model to develop and evaluate comprehensive FSP programs and policies.

Hoover-Dempsey and Sandler

Hoover-Dempsey and Sandler (1995, 1997) have focused their work on understanding why parents choose to become involved in their children's education, on illuminating the importance of different forms of parent involvement, and on further analyses of how parental involvement affects critical student outcomes. Their study of these issues during the elementary and middle school years has helped to illuminate the impact of parental beliefs on decisions about whether to become involved in their child's schooling. Hoover-Dempsey and Sandler have conducted both conceptual and empirical work to better explain the underpinnings of parents' decisions to become involved in their student's education. Most simply, Hoover-Dempsey and Sandler concluded that parental involvement in schools is primarily motivated by parents' beliefs about their roles and their feelings of efficacy related to helping their children succeed in school.

More recently, these researchers have further elucidated five key levels of involvement factors: (a) personal motivation, invitations from the school to be involved, and life context, including time and energy, knowledge, and skills; (b) parent mechanisms of involvement, such as encouragement for schoolwork or modeling behavior; (c) student's perceptions of these parent mechanisms of involvement; (d) student attributes conducive to achievement, including the child's motivation to learn and academic self-efficacy; and (e) student achievement outcomes. Their findings support the need to focus on internal or psychological motivators as well as pragmatic issues that can influence parents' decisions to initiate and sustain involvement in the school. Furthermore, they address the need to understand how children's perceptions of their parents' school-related involvement activities can also influence achievement outcomes and argue that specific invitations from school staff serve as key motivators for parents' ideas about their roles in their children's education and their ultimate decisions to be involved.

Christenson and Sheridan

The model proposed by Christenson and Sheridan (2001) also recognizes the importance of the home and school contexts and strong interpersonal relationships between families and educators that are built on mutual respect and trust. An essential assumption of this model is that authentic family-school partnerships depend on four interrelated elements or essential conditions, known as the "four As." *Approach* elements are policies and interpersonal practices that frame expected relationships and interpersonal interactions between families and school staff. *Attitude* elements are the shared values and perceptions individuals hold about family-school relationships. *Atmosphere* elements refer to physical and interpersonal climate characteristics that make families and students feel welcome and accepted in a school building. Finally, *action* elements are the resulting activities developed at a district or building level to build strong family-school partnerships.

Direct examinations of factors that enable or disable these conditions have been the focus of many studies (Christenson & Sheridan, 2001; Ysseldyke & Christenson, 2002). FSP strategies associated with this model include positive attitudes about partners' intentions, strategies that build trust, and common goals. Home-school relationships that conform to these characteristics have been related to high student scholastic achievement as well as other positive outcomes (Esler, Godber, & Christenson, 2008; Sheldon, 2006). Trust is something that is intentionally built through creating personal relationships with families and committing to focusing on what is best for the student's school success (Adams & Christenson, 2000). In addition, educators must be self-reflective in their attempts to partner with families. Christenson and Sheridan (2001) recommended school professionals consider a host of questions to ask themselves including whether they accept families for who they are, what the tone is that they exude (from warm to aloof), and the extent to which they follow through on their promises to students and families. At the end of the chapter, we include a staff reflection tool that can assist practitioners in reflecting on their FSP efforts.

CREATING CORE FSP PHILOSOPHIES

All four conceptual strands were helpful in creating core FSP philosophies (refer to Table 2.1). From Bronfenbrenner, we learned that the student is always the center of the model, and that the qualities of interactions among systems matter. Epstein reminded us of the importance of applying systems theory specifically to families and school and operationalized theory into specific, concrete practices. Hoover-Dempsey and Sandler tied parent involvement to key student outcomes and focused on the internal motivations and beliefs that can

Table 2.1 Four Conceptual Strands Influencing Family-School Partnering (FSP)

Theorists	Key Ideas Influencing FSP Philosophy
Bronfenbrenner	• Child develops within interrelated systems • Quality of connections and interactions across systems matters (mesosystem) • Reciprocal nature of development (child influences environment and environment influences child)
Epstein	• Six types of parent involvement (parenting, communicating, volunteering, learning at home, decision making, collaborating with community) • Links between theory and actual practices of involvement • Overlap between home and school crucial
Hoover-Dempsey and Sandler	• Focus on why parents become involved in children's schooling • Parents' ideas about their roles in their children's education and their sense of self-efficacy have impact on involvement decisions • Links between parent involvement and key student outcomes
Christenson and Sheridan	• Four interrelated elements affecting parent involvement (approach, attitude, atmosphere, action) • Importance of building trust through personal relationships • Self-reflection regarding partnership

affect FSP. Finally, Christenson and Sheridan highlighted the importance of relationship and building trust and a deepening understanding of context for successful FSP. Taken together, across all conceptual strands we recognize a similar core principle: Families themselves are unique cultures with their own set of belief systems and patterns of interacting. In addition to this idea, it is important to consider the unique cultural systems present in schools to think critically about how to partner across diverse family and school systems.

Cultural Sharing

Cultural sharing allows for families to learn about each school's unique culture and school staff to learn about each family's unique culture. Cultural sharing involves providing information about context, including routines and celebrations, as well as life paths. This is especially important for family members from minority cultures who often feel disenfranchised from the education or other political spheres of influence in the United States (Allen, 2007).

According to the U.S. Bureau of the Census (2004), 60% of the population will be multicultural or bilingual by 2050. To truly embrace the philosophies of FSP, school staff must find ways to connect with each family and learn about the unique culture of each family. Some researchers have argued that requests for traditional family involvement in schools represent a middle-class, suburban model that excludes families with different social and material backgrounds (de Carvalho, 2001). In the past, families of color have been blamed for their children's underachievement and charged with expressing fundamentally low expectations around education (Diamond, Wang, & Gomez, 2004; Stanton-Salazar, 2001).

Too often, families of diverse backgrounds have been unfairly perceived as uncaring or uninvolved in their children's education when the definition of involvement is narrow and constrained to traditional forms of parent involvement (Delgado-Gaitan, 1992). Poverty, too, has been studied as a factor that plays into perceptions of family-school partnering efforts. In general, families living in poverty report fewer feelings of outreach and engagement from schools and tend to be less involved in the cultures of the school (Enyeart, Diehl, Hampden-Thompson & Scotchmer, 2006; Grolnick & Slowiaczek, 1994; Vaden-Kiernan & McManus, 2005). But poverty is not a culture so much as a set of circumstances that can affect both families and schools' resources and their resulting social capital (Lareau, 2003). Poverty also thins resources which may lead to fewer opportunities for traditional family-school partnering activities.

However, emerging research suggests that a solid majority of families of diverse backgrounds and material circumstances care deeply about their children's education (Christenson, 2004; Holloway, Fuller, Rambaud, & Eggers- Piérola, 1997) and attempt to monitor their progress and assist with problems (Stanton-Salazar, 2001; Valdés, 1996; Valenzuela, 1999). For example, many immigrant families see education as a primary form of social mobility and seek to motivate their children to succeed in school through stories of hardship and triumph (Delgado-Gaitan, 1994). Poor schools also find ways to connect with families in the face of marginal resources. Through creative efforts to connect with families despite limited finances, schools have been able to empower and build lasting relationships with the families in their communities (Bryk & Schneider, 2002; Reyes, Scribner, & Scribner, 1999). There is a great need for school professionals to continue to find ways to help families of all backgrounds feel comfortable demonstrating their knowledge and authority about their child (Allen, 2007).

Addressing cultural diversity and poverty within FSP is no simple task. It depends on cultural sharing that honors unique traditions, patterns of interacting, and ways of thinking found within family and school systems. Broadly speaking, *culture* is a shared system of spoken and unspoken values, beliefs, and behaviors transmitted in a variety of ways and passed down from generation to generation within a family, school, or community (Gallimore & Goldenberg, 2001). Cultural sharing occurs when school professionals and families recognize and appreciate each other's cultural background (Garcia Coll & Chatman, 2005; Ortiz, Flanagan, & Dynda, 2008; Sue & Sue, 2003) (please refer to Table 2.2).

To truly partner with families from all different walks of life, it is important to begin with the goal of learning about each family, school context, and funds of knowledge (González & Moll, 2002). One way to do this is through semistructured interviews that are less expert driven, more conversational, and in which both partners learn about each other. We have included a starting point for these conversations through a sociocultural interview, which is included as a tool at the end of the chapter and on the CD. Sharing must occur within a

Table 2.2 Tips for Cultural Sharing

Family Sharing	School Sharing
Share:	Share:
• Beliefs and expectations for education to enhance student school success	• Beliefs and expectations for education to enhance student school success
• Important facets of your culture (e.g., food preferences, affiliations, etc.)	• Important facets of your culture (e.g., expectations, mission, vision, etc.)
• Customs, routines, and rituals important to your family or culture	• Customs, routines, and rituals that make a school/classroom work
• Previous experiences with schooling or schools	• Previous experiences of the school with different cultures
• Hopes and dreams for children's future	• Hopes and dreams for all students' future
• Children's unique strengths, personality, and accomplishments (likes/dislikes)	• Students' unique strengths, persistence, and overall successes

climate of openness and an authentic willingness to invest time in building a relationship. In a true partnership, families and staff are equal partners who share power and status, who feel trusted and respected by the other, and who believe they are working toward similar values and goals. Strong FSP requires a sustained long-term commitment that establishes a bridge between home and school by outlining roles and responsibilities for jointly supporting a child's learning and development.

As a practitioner working in the system of a school, understanding how one's cultural lens and expectations for children are similar and how they differ from families is a first step in cultural sharing. It is important to recognize that the United States' educational system operates very differently than systems found in other countries. The goal is to find commonalities and shared educational beliefs as well as to understand and illuminate critical differences. Initial discussions can focus on finding some common ground by discussing each other's goals and dreams for a specific child. Once common goals are found, then it is important to examine and recognize how one's cultural views about education can differ. Practitioners, families, and students might begin this process by sharing a book or favorite school story together which can lead to a comparison of the US and other educational experiences. This can initiate a more open dialogue about culture and also raise each other's consciousness about what can make it more or less difficult to build family-school partnerships. One book that we found helpful in our process is by Fadiman (1997), *The Spirit Catches You and You Fall Down*. This in turn can engender a deeper understanding of the cultural models of others and a wider view of child development across different contexts. In general, increasing one's cultural literacy, or knowledge of one's own and other cultures' norms, practices, and acculturation, can assist practitioners in identifying potential cultural models and reflecting on their interactions with diverse families (Garcia Coll & Chatman, 2005; Ortiz et al., 2008; Sue & Sue, 2003).

As a family trying to understand the educational system, it is important to understand educators' underlying beliefs and values regarding the education of their students. To assist families in identifying educational cultures, again, discussions and conversations are a good place to start. Sometimes to initiate this process, families may need reminders and prompts that it is acceptable to ask questions and initiate dialogue.

Sociocultural sharing can be easily built into already existing touch points that occur in schools, such as family-teacher conferences, back-to-school nights, and school and classroom cultural sharing events (e.g., multicultural night or international potlucks). Other ideas and tips that can cultivate a climate of cultural sharing can be found in Table 2.2. In the table, *school* refers to the wider school system as well as to individual classroom systems. We have also included wallet reminder cards as a tool to assist families and staff in remembering the core philosophy and vocabulary as they embark on their partnering journey.

Cultural sharing can be difficult for many reasons. It can be time consuming, raise fears about making wrong assumptions, and feel new and overwhelming because of limited training and prior experiences with such approaches. Most families and school staff have not had experiences concerning how to partner with individuals from different cultures. Moreover, cultural sharing is never complete in that it entails lifelong, continuous learning with each new partner. When people are able to live and learn things through their cultural lens, they are allowed to involve their whole self, which ensures that any content being processed is fully experienced (Gee, 2004). Relationships develop within the context of warm, welcoming settings. Partners begin to communicate in an ongoing, back-and-forth fashion. Families and school staff educate one another about their unique cultures. As a result, students view their families as learning and sharing, and student school success benefits greatly.

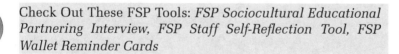

Check Out These FSP Tools: *FSP Sociocultural Educational Partnering Interview, FSP Staff Self-Reflection Tool, FSP Wallet Reminder Cards*

KEY TERMS

- **4 As.** Christenson and Sheridan definition of four interrelated elements affecting parent involvement (approach, attitude, atmosphere, action).
- **Culture.** Shared system of beliefs and behavior, including stories, traditions, ways of thinking, and interacting.
- **Ecological systems theory.** Term originally coined by Urie Bronfenbrenner; describes human development as occurring within interrelated systems.

- **Parent involvement decisions.** Hoover-Dempsey and Sandler's theory that parents' role construction, including their beliefs about their role in their children's education and their feelings of efficacy concerning helping their children succeed in school, influences their decisions to be involved in the school.
- **Philosophy.** Foundation on which all FSP beliefs and actions grow (student school success is the center of FSP, education is a shared responsibility between home and school, families and schools each bring unique expertise and cultures).
- **Six types of parent involvement.** Epstein's components of parenting, communicating, volunteering, learning at home, decision making, and collaborating with community; these were revised by the National PTA in 2009.

TOOL DESCRIPTIONS

FSP Sociocultural Educational Partnering Interview.
These questions can be used flexibly, probably with an
interpreter in a home, to help school staff learn about
a student's life, culture, and family; the tool includes
tips on partnering with interpreters.

FSP Staff Self-Reflection Tool. This personal checklist
can help school staff assess their personal beliefs and
actions concerning FSP.

FSP Wallet Reminder Cards. The two-sided cards for
family members and school staff can be adapted with
specific school information to remind everyone about
practicing FSP.

RESOURCES

Web Sites

*Center on School, Family, and Community
Partnerships:* http://www.csos.jhu.edu/p2000/center.htm

Reports on the research, programs, and policy analyses relating to the National Network of Partnership Schools and other
projects producing scientific knowledge relating to family,
school, and community collaboration.

Family-School Partnership Lab: http://www.
vanderbilt.edu/Peabody/family-school/index.html

Contains published and unpublished papers regarding family-
school partnerships and communication strategies developed
by Hoover-Dempsey and colleagues. Dedicated to the scientific
investigation of the reciprocal relationships among families,
schools, and children.

National Parent Teacher Association: http://www.pta.org

Provides information on parent-teacher organizations, family
and school topics, policy development, and networking.

Books

Christenson, S. L., & Sheridan, S. M. (2001).
*Schools and families: Creating essential connections
for learning.* New York: Guilford Press.

Presents various theories and rationale for family-school partnership, including the four As—approach, atmosphere, attitude, actions—with practical suggestions.

Epstein, J. L., Sanders, M. V., Simon, B. S., Salinas, K. C., Jansorn, N. R., & Van Voorhis, F. L. (2002). *School, family, and community partnerships: Your handbook for action.* Thousand Oaks, CA: Corwin Press.

Maps out a detailed, often-implemented model for developing family partnerships in a school, including relevant research and specific planning tools.

National Parent Teacher Association. (2000). *Building successful partnerships: A guide for developing parent and family involvement programs.* Bloomington, IN: National Educational Services.

Elaborates on each of the original National PTA standards with field-tested ideas from schools across the country. Includes suggestions on forming family-school teams, creating action plans, and overcoming barriers.

Weiss, H. B., Kreider, H., Lopez, M. E., & Chatman, C. M. (2005). *Preparing educators to involve families: From theory to practice.* Thousand Oaks, CA: Sage.

Provides key ecological systems perspectives on FSP with diverse case studies, focus on ecocultural understanding, and practical questions for discussion.

Tools 2.1–2.3

Tool 2.1

Family-School Partnering (FSP)

Sociocultural Educational Partnering Interview

Directions: This is a semistructured interview for families and schools to share information about cultural context and cultural experiences that can have an impact on a student's schooling. Families learn more about their student's classroom and the school culture, and the school learns more about a family's cultural experiences and background. When a student and his or her family are identified as refugees or immigrants, knowledge of the circumstances leading up to that identification is important to understand educational needs and resources, thereby providing essential data for intervention development. This interview should be viewed as two-way communication in which the family and school are encouraged to share information and ask questions that will ensure a student's school success. Broad, open-ended questions and targeted follow-up areas are addressed as appropriate. It is suggested that the interview be conducted by a school mental health professional teamed with an interpreter/cultural liaison. For non-English speakers, it is important to work initially with the interpreter so that the interpreter can understand and explain the rationale for this type of interview and the desire of the school to partner with the family.

- Refugee: A person who is unable or unwilling to return to his/her country because of a well-founded fear of persecution.
- Immigrant: A person who voluntarily comes to a new country.

Student Name: _____ Date: _____
Family Members Interviewed: _____
Interpreter: _____ School Staff: _____

INSTRUCTIONS TO THE FAMILY:

"We are here to learn more about you and _____ (student) and to let you learn more about our school. We believe children will do better in school when families and schools work together (i.e., use words synonymous with partnership here). If we all share our wishes, desires, and hopes for _____ (student) we will better understand how to help _____ (student) succeed. We would like to know more about you and your family but please only respond to questions that are comfortable for you. We also want to be sure that you have a chance to ask us any questions about our school or _____'s (student) classroom or classwork.

(It is very important to take time to be sure that the family understands the purpose of the interview and their choice about answering. They need to know this information is voluntary and will not lead to any harm. It is important to be clear about reporting responsibility as far as danger to self or others, including child abuse. Begin with open-ended questions and follow up on areas as appropriate. The following questions are written for families but can be reframed to use with students.)

Cultural Context

- "Please help us to know more about (family's country of origin)."
- "What was your favorite thing about the country you left?"
- "What things and people do you miss?"

Possible Follow-Up Areas:

- Significant things/customs from home country that they cherished and miss
- Customs or other things they have held onto and one that they are not able to observe
- Connections for student/family with local cultural/religious affiliation
- Support of other extended family members
- Other

Summary/Notes/Comments:

CULTURAL CIRCUMSTANCES

- "Please help us to know more about how you and your family came to the United States."
- "What was it like for you and your family to leave?"
- "What happened once you (had to/decided to) leave?"

Possible Follow-Up Areas:

- Refugees/immigrants or sons/daughters of refugees/immigrants
- Number of moves
- Family members left behind
- Loss of significant family members
- Travel to this new country (e.g., Was it a traumatic experience?)
- Other traumatic events, such as assault, imprisonment, political prosecution, and the like
- Other

Summary/Notes/Comments:

CURRENT FAMILY CONTEXT

- "Please tell us about your family."
- "Where is the birthplace of (student and other family members)?"
- "What was the birth of (student) like?"

Possible Follow-Up Areas:

- Family size and constellation
- Languages spoken in the home
- Birthplace and birth of student and siblings
- Development and medical history of student and other family members

- Sibling and parent relationships
- History of mental illness, developmental disabilities (be sure to explain this since this term is not familiar to many other cultures)

Summary/Notes/Comments:

FAMILY ADJUSTMENT

- "What has been the most difficult thing for you and your family about being here?"
- "What has been the easiest and best thing for your family about being here?"
- "How are schools and education different here from schools and education in your home country?

Possible Follow-Up Areas

- Student/family acculturation
- Family supports/connection/involvement with community
- Parent/family employment
- Accessibility and ease of transportation
- Involvement with the law
- How time is observed in home culture
- Acceptance of Western education
- Acceptance of Western medicine, mental health, and other support

Summary/Notes/Comments:

SCHOOL HISTORY AND STUDENT ADJUSTMENT

- "Tell me about your child's past schooling or schools." (Recognize that for many there may not have been traditional places or opportunities for schooling.)
- "What were teachers like in the past?"
- "Where did (student) attend school?"

- "What things do you or (student name) like and dislike about school here?"
- "How does (student name) get along with others—is this the same/different from before?"
- "What concerns, if any, do you have about (student name)?"

Possible Follow-Up Areas:

- School experiences in past: type of schools attended: rural, urban
- Teachers' prior role in partnering with student and parents
- Attendance in past: regular or irregular
- Transitions in past: feelings and adjustment
- Special education/other services: therapies, medication, tutoring, counseling, and so on
- Peer relationships
- Discipline expectations
- Homework and teacher relationships

Summary/Notes/Comments

STUDENT STRENGTHS AND EDUCATIONAL EXPECTATIONS

- "Tell us more about (student name): What is (he or she) good at, what are you proud of?"
- "What does (student name) like to do?"
- "What are your hopes and dreams for the future for (student name)?"

Possible Follow-Up Areas:

- Strengths of student
- Personality, behaviors, coping style, independence, self-advocacy skills
- General health, developmental milestones, prior hospitalizations
- Access to television and computer time

- Peer relationships: younger, older, stability, positive, negative
- Any concerns about prior danger: suicidal thinking, self-harm, and so on
- Outside/extracurricular activities: clubs, sports, volunteering
- Student responsibilities at home
- Family rules and discipline

Summary/Notes/Comments:

SOLICIT FAMILY INPUT AND INCREASE CONFIDENCE IN PARTNERING

- "I am sure there are many things you want to know about our school."
- "We want you to know it is important for us to find ways that will make it easy to communicate. We want you to get answers and information that will let you feel more comfortable with your child's education here."
- "What would you like to know more about regarding our school or your child's classroom or classwork?"
- "What would make it easier for you to get the information you need to help (student name)?"
- "What is the best way for us to communicate?"
- "How often would you like to get together to talk about (student's name) progress?"
- "What did I not ask you about that would be good for me to know about you and your student?"

Summary/Notes/Comments:

Recommendations/Suggestions/Plans/Next Steps:

Family Contact Information:

HELPFUL INTERVIEW AND INTERPRETER TIPS

These suggestions and ideas can make the interpretation/translation process more successful in partnering interviews.

Environment

- Make sure all participants feel comfortable.
- Limit, if possible, the interview to the smallest number of people.
- Seating arrangements are critical; let family members choose where to sit if possible.
- Arrange seating so that all participants can maintain eye contact with each other.
- Be sure the interpreter never blocks the family from others.
- Be sure all professionals directly address the family, not the interpreter.
- Introductions are important; give names and the role and position of each person present in relationship to the child.

Timing

- Give family a time reference for the interview.
- Be sure there is enough time since interpretation requires extra time.
- Share ideas for how and who will keep time during the interview.

Listening

- Maintain a responsive posture that indicates full attention to each speaker.
- Remember that body language can cue acceptance and openness to questions.
- If recording, explain what will be recorded and how the information will be used.

Values/Attitudes

- Be aware of attitudes that are displayed since these can set the tone of the conference.
- Be sensitive to individual differences across all ethnic groups and avoid stereotyping.
- Be aware of language and tribal differences within ethnic groups.
- Assume the family member understands more than he or she acknowledges.

Authority

- The interpreter should not "editorialize" any comments made by school personnel or family members.
- Remember to remain neutral.
- The goal is to get all participants to feel understood and to form a united team.

Closing Remarks

- The school professional in charge should make the closing remarks and summarize.
- Be sure time is taken to elicit final questions and to discuss a follow-up plan.
- Thank everyone for his/her input.
- Reassure the family that the information they shared was helpful and welcomed.

Tool 2.2

Family-School Partnering (FSP)

Staff Self-Reflection Tool

DO I ... ?

- Connect with every family soon after school begins?
- Personally always start with a positive message?
- Talk about my desire to work together to help the student?
- Express the fact that family members' input and perspective are important?
- Convey respect for family members as experts on their child?
- Identify the circumstances under which families feel more or less comfortable and try to understand those feelings?
- Approach families flexibly, offering multiple times, places, and modalities?
- Elicit, openly value, and use families' input?
- Ask open-ended questions to get families' full thoughts?
- Really listen to family members?
- Thank the families for listening, caring, and helping?
- Tell students that I am partnering with their families?
- Always use two-way communication, asking for family ideas, not just sharing my own?
- Productively problem solve concerns so each student is successful?
- Provide ideas about homework and various approaches that can support learning at home?

HOW CAN I ... ?

- Use partnering language to promote teaming? For example,
  - Use common language ("us," "we," "let's")
  - Use family members' words
  - Convey understanding
- Ask the parent for help in a respectful, mutually gratifying way?
- Clarify responsibilities of each person?

- Avoid advice giving?
- Meet parents "on their turf"?
- Make events fun?
- Make sure roles are meaningful?
- Plan for and prevent logistical barriers?
- Make time to build relationships with all families?
- Gain confidence in my ability to talk comfortably with families?
- Learn about the unique culture of each family?

Source: Adapted from Future of School Psychology Task Force on Family-School Partnerships. *Family-school partnership training modules,* 2007. Retrieved March 31, 2009, from http://fsp.unl.edu/future_index.htm.

Tool 2.3

Family-School Partnering (FSP)

Wallet Reminder Cards

FAMILY-SCHOOL PARTNERING (FSP)

1. Student school success is the center of family-school partnering.
2. Education is a shared responsibility between home and school.
3. Families and educators each bring unique expertise and cultures.

FAMILIES, STUDENTS, AND STAFF
FSP TIPS

- Use partnering words: *we, our, us, shared, partner, together*
- Build relationships
- Create welcoming settings
- Use two-way communication
- Educate partners
- Use team interventions

Name and Contact Information: _____

Source: Adapted from Colorado Department of Education. *Family and community partnering: "On the team and at the table,"* Author, Denver, CO, 2009.

Three

Creating Universal FSP Processes and Practices

The missing piece of the proficiency puzzle is involving families and communities in improving student
achievement.

Adapted from Kentucky Department of Education, 2007

Chapter 3 is devoted to a review of four universal family-
school partnering (FSP) processes inherent in all universal FSP
efforts that support the other tiers. Field-documented practices
associated with each of the four processes are described with
references to resources for further information. We provide
universal support for the FSP definition: *Family-school partnering is sharing responsibility for a student's school success.*
    After reviewing this chapter, the reader will

- Understand four processes that should permeate all
  universal FSP efforts
- Conceptualize major practices that contribute to these
  four processes
- Relate universal processes and practices to student
  school success and coordinated learning

The primary goal of FSP at the universal level is to create a
unified partnering climate so that families and educators recognize their vested interest in helping all children succeed.
A universal partnering approach rests on the foundational
beliefs outlined in Chapter 2; the focus of shared responsibility between home and school is a student's school success.
The universal tier represents global and pervasive processes
that should be in place for all stakeholders. When universal
FSP processes prevail, 80–90% of families, students, and staff
will flourish and express feelings of engagement and shared

responsibility. Universal processes not only mitigate the need for but also underlie FSP at the upper tiers.

At least four essential universal processes set the stage for families and educators to work together, coordinating learning for student school success. These four universal processes can be viewed as the building blocks or the "core curriculum" of a successful home-school partnership. They are intended to *build relationships, create welcoming settings, provide two-way communication,* and *educate partners.* Strong working relationships are built by showing respect, taking time to partner, and recognizing all partnering efforts. Welcoming settings are created by addressing environmental factors and recognizing alternative ways that families support education. Two-way communication is promoted when a variety of communication options are available that stress the positive and encourage responses from all partners. Educated partners share critical knowledge that leads to increased confidence in one's ability to nurture a student's development.

These processes serve as a conceptual framework for the creation and evaluation of individualized and sustainable school-wide FSP. Similar universal processes are embedded in the recently revised national standards for parent/family involvement (National Parent Teacher Association [PTA], 2009); in recommendations forwarded by the National Family, School, and Community Engagement Working Group (2009); and in the guidelines developed across FSP researchers (Patrikakaou, Weissberg, Redding, & Walberg, 2005). Such universal FSP efforts should be a part of annual school performance indicators and staff performance evaluations. Weaving FSP into the fabric of the school overcomes the tendency to select a hodgepodge of family involvement activities that are not fully integrated into everyday school routines and practices. A slide presentation for school staff and families, explaining these universal processes and practices, has been designed for adaptable site use.

Check Out This FSP Tool: *FSP Universal Stakeholder Slides*

Excellent compendiums of universal FSP practices associated with each of these processes have been published (Epstein, 2001; Epstein & Sanders, 2002; Henderson et al., 2007). Thus, the goal of this chapter is not to replicate this work but rather to highlight essential characteristics of everyday home and school practices associated with these processes. Several examples of successful practices are provided rather than an exhaustive list since it is our belief that FSP efforts at the universal tier must be strategically selected and adapted to meet the unique characteristics of each school community. Indeed, universal practices should systematically meet the needs of each school and classroom. Those chosen should be based on a clear rationale and review of schoolwide data, jointly determined goals, and the likelihood of sustainability over the long term. Comprehensive planning frameworks have been developed to assist in this endeavor and give families a strong voice in planning universal FSP efforts (Ellis & Hughes, 2002; Henderson et al., 2007). Additional resources and Web links to universal practices are provided at the end of the chapter.

BUILD RELATIONSHIPS

Strong FSP relationships are fostered by showing respect, taking the time to partner, and recognizing partnering efforts. FSP is more likely when trusting relationships are built between school staff, family members, and students (Christenson & Godber, 2001). Student achievement and engagement is enhanced when FSP is viewed as a beneficial relationship for all (Esler et al., 2008). To promote such relationships, there must be an atmosphere of respectful collaboration so that families believe their voices will be heard (Christenson, 2004; Pianta & Walsh, 1996). Mapp (2003) has identified the significance of "joining" to promote home-school relationships. Joining occurs when families and educators assume positive intentions, demonstrate mutual respect, acknowledge each other's contributions, and trust that each partner will go out of his or her way to help and follow through.

The importance of taking a family perspective, holding positive impressions of, empathizing with, and recognizing the enduring and central role of families in students' lives are critical characteristics of family-centered principles (Dunst, Trivette, & Deal, 2003). According to these researchers, strong relationships with families depend on relational and participatory skills that include one's attitude toward working with families, active and empathic listening, responsiveness to family priorities, and the ability to promote and assist families in their choices (Dunst, 2002; Wilson & Dunst, 2002).

Relationships that incorporate these principles promote family strengths, confidence, and resources, which further enable family members to play a central role in their child's educational success (Sheridan, Taylor, & Woods, 2008).

In a similar vein, "courageous conversations" have been identified as a critical element of nationally recognized parental involvement efforts (Henderson, 2001; Henderson & Berla, 1994). Such conversations occur when educators and families listen to and share each other's hopes and dreams for their children so that each partner gains a better appreciation of the other's educational beliefs, role expectations, and child management preferences (Henderson & Mapp, 2002). Indeed, the goal of these conversations is to ensure that all partners feel acknowledged for what they bring to the table to support a student's success. Families bring intimate knowledge of student needs and talents and an enduring interest in their child's future. Educators bring intimate knowledge of curriculum content and an enduring interest in teaching and motivating students to ensure their long-term success.

Efforts to assess family perspectives of a child's strengths, interests, and behavior also are powerful transmitters of respect that can lead to more culturally responsive FSP environments (Ortiz et al., 2008). Relationships are enhanced when school and family partners share cultural traditions and assumptions about schooling, openly acknowledge their stage of acculturation, and move beyond race and ethnicity to appreciate diversity within groups regarding personal values, beliefs, and biases (Jones, 2009). Respectful understanding is created when there is acceptance that people have different perspectives and that each partner deserves an equal voice.

It is important to understand that such relationships take time to develop and must be nurtured through nonrushed, face-to-face sharing opportunities. However, time is a precious commodity for school staff and family members. Thus, a first step in universal FSP planning is to determine how relationships might be enhanced during already established meeting and conference times. Relationship building is especially critical when a child first enters formal schooling and during transitions to a new school or district (Jeynes, 2005). Some researchers also stress that relational factors may play an even larger role in predicting school success as a student transitions into middle and high school (Barnard, 2004; Bridgeland et al., 2008). A relationship can be more difficult to cultivate if families or educators have had negative experiences in the

Table 3.1 FSP Concepts, Vocabulary, and Sample Phrases

Concept	Vocabulary	Sample Phrases
A student focus	Our, we, us	What is best for *our* student?
A family's perspective	Believe, think, feel	What do you *believe, think, feel* about this?
Goals for success	Achieve together	What do we hope to *achieve together?*
Joint roles	Partner	How can we *partner* around this?
Collaborative decision making	On the team—at the table	We are *on the same team (at the same table).*
Shared responsibility	Each of us	What can *each of us* do before our next meeting?

past or when partners' sense of efficacy is relatively weak (Henderson, 2001). Efficacy deals with feelings that one is capable of helping a child learn as well as individuals feeling confident in their ability to partner with one another. In such cases, specific individual invitations to partner may be needed from students, from trusted school or community members, or from other parent leaders (Hoover-Dempsey & Sandler, 1997). Indeed, researchers have found that parent perceptions of invitations to partner have a strong influence on subsequent decisions to become and stay involved in their children's education (Hoover-Dempsey et al., 2005).

Finally, all efforts, no matter how small, that help to build relations must be recognized, supported, and continually evaluated for their impact throughout the year and through systems of professional performance evaluation. It is especially helpful for partners to develop a common, universal FSP vocabulary. Families, educators, and community members will succeed more often when they are continually encouraged and reinforced for using vocabulary that stresses their work together. See Table 3.1 for several examples of critical FSP vocabulary and phrases that should be a part of all student-focused discussions between staff and families.

Practices to Build Relationships: Show Respect, Take Time, and Recognize Efforts

- Early in the year, send welcome back letters that not only introduce families to the school and classroom but also invite families and students to share personal interests, ideas, and future dreams and to discuss what they need to ensure their student's success.

- Plan schoolwide or classroom activities to share various interests, talents, and traditions and ask students to invite family members to these special events.
- Establish flexible hours for home or other face-to-face visits that allow staff and families to get to know each other and ask each family to get to know and call at least one new family during the year.
- Reformat already-established meeting times like back-to-school nights or parent-teacher conferences so that the focus is on building a relationship with families and spending time to get to know each other (e.g., get-to-know-you back-to-school nights, classroom open houses led by students, potlucks with students and families, caring community events, and fun nights for the whole family).
- Throughout the year, extend personal invitations to partner, use words that promote partnership (us, we, let's), and find ways to honor all contributions by staff, family, and community members who exemplify strong FSP (e.g., special events such as people-who-make-a-difference day, my-male-hero day, "you-are-a-star" notes).

Check Out These FSP Tools: *FSP Principal Two-Way Welcome Letter/Newsletter, FSP Teacher Two-Way Welcome Letter, FSP Family Sharing Sheet*

CREATE WELCOMING SETTINGS

Families are more likely to participate in their child's education when they feel welcomed and connected to the school and their child's teachers (Ellis & Hughes, 2002). Welcoming settings depend on strong relationships as well as the physical and structural environment. As a first step, it is critically important to take stock of all physical contact points in a school (e.g., building exterior, entrances, front office, hallway displays, classroom doorways). This should also include an analysis of structural factors that help create psychologically inviting climates (Dauber & Epstein, 1993). Families are more likely to enter a building perceived as well organized, safe, and attractive (Connors & Epstein, 1995). Schools also are perceived as more inviting when there are schoolwide and classroom displays that demonstrate acceptance of different family cultures and family structures (Ortiz et al., 2008).

Another feature of a welcoming school is the type of reception provided by front office staff. Greetings from front office and other school personnel must be considered critical initial contact points that can have a strong impact on a family's perception of school friendliness and on subsequent decisions to be involved at the school. Constantino (2003) has suggested that family members and any other guests who enter the building be treated as a guest or as a "valuable customer." He also suggests that time should be taken to assess each guest's satisfaction after every visit. A guest response tool is provided at the end of this chapter.

Additional variables that can foster family engagement are having convenient and clearly publicized ways to contact and access staff. When staff, teachers, and administrators take time to routinely listen and respond to families, satisfaction with school increases (Epstein, Sanders et al., 2002). Establishing a designated place in the school where families can gather, network, and gain helpful educational information or community resources also has been found to lead to more frequent participation at school meetings and events (Henderson et al., 2007; Miller & Choy, 2009).

Welcoming settings also recognize the variety of ways that families support a child's education. Traditionally, educators perceive families more favorably when they are visibly present at the school to volunteer, fund-raise, or attend conferences or school functions (Epstein & Becker, 1982; Izzo, Weissberg, Kasprow, & Fendrich, 1999). However, when visible rather than less-visible family presence and contributions are stressed, many families will be unable to participate due to economic constraints, inflexible employment hours, or a lack of self-confidence (Hoover-Dempsey et al., 2005). This can create a cycle that increases the likelihood of continued involvement in families who already feel more comfortable educationally, while lessening that of others who may not feel as comfortable in school settings (Pomerantz, Grolnick, & Price, 2005). Indeed, limited English language proficiency and prior educational experiences can lower parental confidence about how to have an impact on their child's education (Delgado Gaitan, 2004). It is unclear how many "nonengaged" families may stay away from school because they feel that the personal knowledge they bring about their child will be diminished because it does not match that of the institution (White, 2009).

To enhance FSP at the universal level, there must be clear recognition of the many nontraditional or less-visible home and community activities that support learning (Seginer, 2006) so that visible involvement is not perceived as more important than the lived practices of the family (Klassen-Endrizzi, 2004). In recent years, there has been more recognition of the importance of out-of-school learning. The term *coordinated learning* has been used to describe the concept of connecting a student's home and school worlds and supporting learning outside school to equalize academic opportunities between affluent students and those experiencing poverty (Clark, 2002). Partnerships are more fully legitimized when both parties learn to value and honor the literate schooling that occurs on a regular functional basis at home (Hicks, 2002). Important paradigm shifts must occur to begin a true partnership of sharing, listening, and learning from and with each other on a regular basis (Allen, 2007). This is especially important for disenfranchised family members, who must be empowered to show or explain the knowledge about their child that their family brings to the table. Educators must extend clear invitations to families, but to act on these, family members must feel welcomed and confident that their input and ideas will be valued and heard (Delgado Gaitan, 2004).

Marzano (2003), after an extensive review of the school effectiveness literature, identified the home environment as one of the top factors influencing achievement. Student achievement was highest in families who reported frequent and systematic discussions about school or schoolwork; who routinely supervised homework, TV viewing, and afterschool activities; and who communicated high expectations within a warm and supportive environment. Based on this review, Marzano (2003) recommended that schools develop effective venues where families could learn about positive home support strategies.

Families benefit from knowing that they support education when, at home, they make positive comments about school, demonstrate interest in and awareness of school activities, converse about current events, discuss their own educational values and aspirations, encourage high achievement expectations, and monitor afterschool activities and homework

(Manz, Fantuzzo, & Power, 2004; Zhang, Miller, Ani, & Chen, 2009). Such "invisible" home support activities relate to positive ratings of involvement as reported by students, parents, and teachers (Mantzicopoulos, 2003; Seginer, 2006) and are stronger predictors of a child's achievement, language, and literacy skills and teachers' perceptions of a child's school abilities than traditional markers that stress a family's presence at the school (Hess, Holloway, Dickson, & Price, 1984; Sénéchal & LeFevre, 2002). The role of nonresident parents—especially fathers—also must be recognized (Amato & Gilbreth, 1999) since increases in student achievement have been reported when fathers' roles and efforts are promoted (Fagan & Palm, 2003; Flouri, 2005; McBride, Schoppe-Sullivan, & Ho, 2005; Pleck & Masciadrelli, 2004). Thus, the key to creating welcoming settings is to acknowledge a broad array of family contributions while overcoming physical and structural barriers to partnering (McWayne, Hampton, Fantuzzo, Cohen, & Sekino, 2004).

Practices to Create Welcoming Settings: Address Environments and Recognize Alternative Contributions

- Greet all families as guests, in their own language; post welcome and location signs in multiple locations; display a map of the school that includes pictures and names of key staff members; and list how to contact all staff members and interpreters
- Assess perceptions of critical contact points, such as the entrance to the school, office, hallways, and classrooms in terms of lighting, attractiveness, safety, and cultural acceptance; assess guests' satisfaction after each visit through a service response card
- Hold informal meetings at various times and locations to listen to and discuss topics of interest to families; designate a place where families can network and access information or resources; find ways to offer child care for families who want to volunteer, visit, or attend school functions
- Develop ways to share information with families who cannot participate, possibly by posting minutes, audio- or videotaping meetings and events, or creating a phone tree by which families who did attend can volunteer to call others who did not

- Widely disseminate and advertise a variety of "less-visible," yet important, ways family members and educators can support the school and a student's learning, possibly through school success pledges

Check Out These FSP Tools: *FSP Guest Response Card, FSP School Success Pledge*

USE TWO-WAY COMMUNICATION

Successful FSP thrives on timely, two-way communication in which information is equally shared between home and school (Walker, Hoover-Dempsey, Whetsel, & Green, 2004). In two-way communication, educators and families feel free to disclose insights, expectations, frustrations, and celebrations related to student achievement and behavior (Christenson & Sheridan, 2001). Such two-way communication contributes to greater student gains and parental satisfaction with teachers and their child's schooling. In a review of research on effective schools, Marzano (2003) found that schools with high student achievement levels also reported more frequent and positive interaction between home and school. Notably, the families at these schools also indicated more regular communication at home with their children about school.

Unfortunately, the results of many nationally published surveys indicated that families are less than satisfied with the communication they have with their child's school or teacher. A consistent finding was that parents reported that they would like more frequent and varied forms of communication (Miller & Kraft, 2008). However, the quality versus the quantity of communication may be a more significant factor in family-school partnerships (Christenson & Sheridan, 2001; Epstein, 2001). Parents' qualitative ratings of satisfaction with teacher communication more strongly predict improvements in children's behavior and academic achievement than the frequency or number of times there is communication (Izzo et al., 1999). In a study with middle school students, standardized test scores were highest in classrooms where teachers reported more communication with parents and where parents reported a healthy partnership with their child's teacher (Clark, 2002). Family members and teachers also hold more positive views of each other when they each feel they are kept abreast of critical home and classroom issues (Epstein et al., 2002; Henderson & Mapp, 2002).

Such findings suggest that traditional unidirectional conferences and end-of-quarter written reports may need to be supplemented, reformatted, or adapted to meet different family preferences, issues, and availability. Indeed, no single communication system has been found to suit everyone's needs. Family preferences regarding how to best communicate also may change over time. During elementary school, families prefer personal face-to-face contact with teachers and opportunities to network and communicate with other parents. While home-school communication is still desired during middle and high school, levels of face-to-face contact decrease, and parents and students report that they prefer telephone calls, electronic mail, and personalized notices (Simon, 2001). Nevertheless, across all age levels, parents who report that they feel included in child-focused school decisions are more likely to rate the school more favorably and to be rated by teachers as more involved in their child's education (Henderson & Mapp, 2002).

Personal outreach and invitations to partner must be intentional and well planned, especially during transition years (Bridgeland et al., 2008). At the secondary level, there is a clear positive correlation among outreach, communication, and family involvement that also leads to higher student achievement and school completion. However, fostering strong FSP in high school is challenging because there are many more students per teacher and more complex subject matter. Teachers also feel that they have less time to devote to individual students and families, and students are learning to balance independence with a continued need for adult guidance and support. Yet, in middle and high school, families still need and desire information on how to further support their student's success.

Two-way homework assignments have led to improved communication between home and school. Such interactive assignments also help students to practice learned skills in different ways and to apply learned knowledge in the real world that reinforces and expands conceptual understanding and supports knowledge transfer and generalization. One example for how this can be done is to create a homework page with a place for family members to add comments or questions about the assignment. Another two-way homework strategy is called "teach to learn." In this approach, a student's assignment is to "teach" a family member a specific skill or content area learned in class. After participating in the lesson, the family member then writes a short summary of what was learned and rates their impression of the "teacher." This allows a student to demonstrate and practice a skill, gives family members a way to learn what is taught at school, and provides critical feedback to the teacher. A third interactive homework strategy is when students and family members collaborate on an interesting topic studied in school. Interactive dialogues fostered through such assignments have been found to lead to improvements in family involvement and student achievement (Epstein, Simon, & Salinas, 1997).

Communication between home and school also is enhanced when family members receive balanced information about their student's strengths and weaknesses that is jargon free and easy to understand. FSP is fostered when schools and families take time to regularly share positive messages and ensure that family members and teachers feel their contributions are valued (Salinas & Jansorn, 2004). More positive than negative school messages should be sent home since negative comments may make a more lasting and harmful impression (Dunst & Trivette, 1987; Constantino, 2003). The degree to which parents perceive school and teacher outreach efforts as constructive and welcoming is an important determinant of school participation decisions (Patrikakou & Weissberg, 2000). Overall, there is strong evidence that favorably perceived, open, two-way communication between parents and school staff is associated with greater family participation in student learning, more satisfaction with school, and higher achievement outcomes (Esler et al., 2008; Henderson & Mapp, 2002; Weiss & Stephen, 2010).

Practices for Two-Way Communication: Offer Options, Focus on Positives, and Invite Responses

- Solicit family feedback about communication preferences and satisfaction; post regular times for families to drop in, call, or contact staff; offer home or community visits, extending invitations to other family members or key family support people
- Develop a 24-hour contact line or a secure password link so that families can leave messages, arrange for meetings, access up-to-date information on their child's progress, or find out about scheduled events and activities

Table 3.2   Family-School Partnering (FSP) Good News Two-Way
Postcard

Good News!

Schools, families, and students partnering for school
success!

Date: November 12, 2010
It makes me proud to tell you that your student accomplished ...
Sarah has completed every class assignment this week, even the most difficult ones.

Sincerely, MS. SNYDER

Let us know what you think... *This is great news! Thanks for sharing.*

Please share some news about your child and return this card to us: *Sarah talked
about school activities every day this week when she arrived home.
She seems to be excited about what she is learning.*

Source: Adapted from Meadow Point Elementary School, Aurora, Colorado, 2009.

- Regularly contact families about a child's strengths
  and progress through "good news" notes that can be
  filled out at staff meetings and set a certain ratio of
  good to bad news contact for all teachers and staff
  members (see Table 3.2 for an example)
- Design interactive home-school assignments with
  fun yet informative activities that are completed with
  a family member and that are connected to learning
  the curriculum
- Establish flexible hours so that staff can spend a
  certain percentage of the week engaged in regular
  personal and positive contact with families; discuss
  FSP at faculty meetings; keep logs of all communication strategies

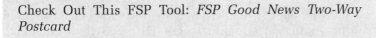

Check Out This FSP Tool: *FSP Good News Two-Way
Postcard*

EDUCATE PARTNERS

A strong partnership must begin with the assumption that all families want to increase their understanding and confidence about how to support their child's achievement (Christenson & Godber, 2001; National PTA, 1998). All parents, even those rated as less engaged by teachers, indicate a strong desire to stay involved in their student's schooling, but many do not know what to do at home (Dauber & Epstein, 1993; Miedel & Reynolds, 1999). Parents, regardless of educational level, income status, or ethnic background, want their children to be successful in school and want more information about how schools function, about children's development/learning, and how to best support their child's education (Christenson, 1995). It also is clear, based on many years of research, that specific things families do facilitate learning and educational success more than who families are in terms of social class, spoken language in the home, or parents' educational level (Christenson & Sheridan, 2001).

Henderson et al. (2007) have studied what motivates parents to support a child's learning and what motivates teachers to engage with parents. These researchers suggested that such motivation is more likely when each partner (a) has received a clear invitation to be engaged, (b) feels that his or her ideas will be welcomed and respected, (c) is confident in his or her ability to help, and (d) knows how to support a child's learning or, in the case of teachers, how to engage parents. Similarly, Hoover-Dempsey and colleagues have studied why parents become involved in their child's education (Hoover-Dempsey & Sandler, 1997; Hoover-Dempsey et al., 2005). Their findings point to the importance of understanding how parents view their roles, knowing how confident parents feel about helping their child learn, and acknowledging parents' perceptions of invitations about being involved. Epstein and colleagues have found that parents more often decide to become involved when they recognize the importance of home support and know how to provide such support (Epstein & Sanders, 2002; Epstein et al., 2002).

Researchers have long recognized the critical need to educate families about the role they play in a young child's school readiness and educational success (Hill, 2001; Powell, 1993). More recently, the critical role of the family during adolescence has been stressed (Hill et al., 2004). Families benefit from knowing that they can positively support schooling during daily routines and through daily expressions of affection, consistent monitoring of afterschool activities, and praising their children for persistence and effort more than final grades (Seginer, 2006). Achievement gains in children are observed when parents are taught how to support learning by talking and reading with a child (Jordan, Snow, & Porche, 2000; Pleck & Masciadrelli, 2004).

Families who feel more confident in their knowledge of child development, parenting, and behavioral guidance and who have high self-efficacy in their ability to help their child learn also have children who are rated higher on self-regulation, self-control, self-competence, and self-esteem, all of which have a strong impact on school achievement (Grolnick et al., 1991; Hoover-Dempsey et al., 2005). Miedel and Reynolds (1999) found that families who feel informed and confident about how to support a child's learning are more willing to communicate and provide feedback to teachers. Building such personal efficacy is especially important when families have limited or negative prior educational experiences (Dearing, Kreider, Simpkins, & Weiss, 2006). Efforts that increase family members' competence and confidence about their ability to help their child in school have included video demonstrations, teacher modeling, and open conversations with other parents. Such efforts have been consistently linked to greater child outcomes (Sheridan et al., 2008; Weiss, Caspe, & Lopez, 2006).

Positive child outcomes also are observed when families feel they understand grade-level expectations and know how to enhance learning at home. Families often desire and require more information about specific curriculum and instructional methods, especially in regard to time management, homework, and how to increase motivation for success (Grolnick et al., 1991; Fishel & Ramirez, 2005). Parents' confidence about supporting their child improves when they receive specific information about how to establish home environments that foster student learning. Such information might include how to create good study routines and habits, how to foster note taking, and how to help a child access or use important resources. Families also benefit from information on how to monitor and discuss homework, how much help to give, and how to reward persistence (Jordan et al., 2000), especially around homework. Indeed, homework has been described as the "linchpin in the relationship between home and school" (Gill, & Schlossman, 2003, p. 846). Secondary-level families also benefit from knowing how to equip their student for the future and how to provide feedback to teachers about difficulties with assignments (Bridgeland et al., 2008).

Teachers desire and benefit from education on how to communicate and collaborate with families, especially during family-teacher conferences (Stevens & Tollafield, 2003). To enhance partnering, teachers need to recognize the contributions families already make and must learn how to ask families about what information and resources they need to further support their child at home. When parents receive ideas from teachers in the context of also getting recognition for how they already support their child, they are more confident about helping with learning at home and rate teachers as more helpful and supportive and the school more favorably (Christenson & Sheridan, 2001; Esler et al., 2008). Teachers who encourage families to request more information about the curriculum and classroom assignments also report more successful sharing of ideas about home-school approaches to enhance a student's success (McWayne et al., 2004; Scott-Jones, 1995).

Consistent, continuous, complementary, and well-coordinated communication and partnering efforts between homes and schools will ensure greater student success. Student improvements at school occur when teachers and family members feel confident about asking each other questions about a child's learning and struggles (Sheridan et al., 2008). Such open conversations enable teachers and families to gain the knowledge and confidence to make informed schoolwide as well as individual student decisions (Davies, 2001). When families feel informed about school requirements and expectations, they are more able to participate and collaborate on school improvement and FSP efforts (Rothman, 2007).

Practices to Educate Partners: Cultivate Shared Understanding and Increase Confidence

- Offer curriculum demonstration lessons for families; videotape lessons or send home iPod lessons that allow a child to "take my teacher home"; and establish a home lending library with grade-level texts, curriculum guides, and other school learning resources
- Create a homework resource hotline; send examples of completed homework with scoring guides; develop handouts with homework ideas and answers to frequently asked questions

- Offer joint staff and family workshops (i.e., "What Every Parent/Teacher Wants to Know") or partnering academies designed to enhance decision making, advocacy, and collaboration; be sure to provide transportation, child care, and interpreters when necessary; take time to elicit and discuss perceived differences between home and school culture and the importance of partnering in U.S. schools, especially with families who may have limited contact with the educational system, who may have just entered our country, or who may have had very different prior schooling experiences
- Have translated materials readily available for families and offer interpreter services whenever a family needs to communicate with or get information about the school, not only during conferences; avoid any communication that might be taken as defining children and families from different cultures in unfamiliar or defict ways

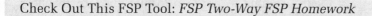

Check Out This FSP Tool: *FSP Two-Way FSP Homework*

KEY TERMS

- **Building relationships:** Developing trusting, positive family-school relationships by taking time, showing respect, and recognizing partnering efforts.
- **Coordinated learning:** Linking in- and out-of-school learning for students to increase generalization, practice, and expansion opportunities.
- **Creating welcoming settings**: Building comfortable surroundings and acceptance for families by addressing the environment and recognizing alternative contributions.
- **Educating partners**: Home and school participants learn together by cultivating shared understanding and increasing confidence.
- **Universal tier:** Welcoming processes and practices to support partnering for all students, families, and staff; these efforts are effective for 80–90% of a school community.
- **Using two-way communication**: Mutually sharing information between home and school by offering options, focusing on positives, and inviting responses.

TOOL DESCRIPTIONS

- *FSP Universal Stakeholder Slides.* Our training slides present the four basic universal FSP processes, with suggested practices that school staff and families can implement in their everyday interactions around students (CD only).

Building Relationships
- *FSP Principal Two-Way Welcome Letter/Newsletter.* The letter sample provides words that focus on FSP for student success and includes an invitation to respond with family feedback.
- *FSP Teacher Two-Way Welcome Letter.* The letter sample provides words that focus on FSP for student success, including communicating around homework, and includes an invitation to respond with family feedback.
- *FSP Family Sharing Sheet.* Families, including the student, are able to share information with teachers using this sheet.

Creating Welcoming Settings
- *FSP Guest Response Card.* An adaptable tool for sites to have available any time families visit the school for any reason, this card is an easy way to access FSP feedback.
- *FSP School Success Pledge.* Teachers, families, and students can review and sign this pledge to focus partnering efforts on coordinating learning.

Using Two-Way Communication
- *FSP Good News Two-Way Postcard.* This is a simple two-way communication tool to share positive news about a student between home and school.

Educating Partners
- *FSP Two-Way Homework.* The importance of family-school communication about homework is described in this tool for teachers.

RESOURCES
Web Sites
National Center on Fathers and Families:
http://www.healthfinder.gov/orgs/hr2906.htm

Serves as a resource for the participation of fathers in children's lives; disseminates research that advances the understanding of father involvement.

TIPS: Teachers Involve Parents in Schoolwork:
http://www.csos.jhu.edu/p2000/tips/index.htm

Provides research and practical guidance in developing interactive homework.

Books
Constantino, S. M. (2003). *Engaging all families: Creating a positive school culture by putting research into practice.* Lanham, MD: Scarecrow Education.

Describes how to begin supporting schools in working with families. From the experience of a high school principal, focuses specifically on leadership and includes basic checklist of actions.

Constantino, S. M. (2008). *101 ways to create real family engagement.* Galax, VA: ENGAGE! Press.

Provides practical, field-tested ideas on how school staff and families can work together.

Dunst, C. J., Trivette, C. M., & Deal, A. G. (2003). *Enabling and empowering families: Principles and guidelines for practice.* Newton, MA: Brookline Books.

Shares theory and research regarding family-centered practices, including rationale and implementation efforts.

Henderson, A. T., Mapp, K. L., Johnson, V. R., & Davies, D. (2007). *Beyond the bake sale: The essential guide to family-school partnerships.* New York: New Press.

Provides conceptual and practical information for educators wanting to understand and apply family-partnering information from the classroom to community to policy. Includes sample tools for various stakeholders.

Tools 3.1–3.7

Tool 3.1

Family-School Partnering (FSP)

Principal Two-Way Welcome Letter/Newsletter

Date _____

Dear Families,

Welcome back to school! We are looking forward to a year of learning and partnership. We are committed to helping every student succeed in school. Specifically, I want to share some important focus areas we will be addressing in the upcoming months. We want to clearly communicate our beliefs about partnering with families. We would like to share some of our ideas and invite your input on this important topic.

At _____ (school), we believe it is important for families and schools to work together and share responsibility for student success. We very much value family members' expertise about their children. Families know a student best, and we can learn from you. Also, we want our students to know the importance of schools and families partnering together to support their work at school. As part of this goal, we have developed some two-way communication tools that can be shared between your home and our school. You will be hearing more about these in the next few weeks. They are (include school-specific activities; the following are examples)

- Classroom two-way communication tools (these vary by teacher and grade or department) so that you and your student's teacher can share successes and concerns at both home and school in an ongoing manner.
- Classroom expectations for homework, behavior, and learning communicated to you by your student. We want students to know and understand that we are working with you to help them succeed. Your student's teacher will follow up to see if you have questions.
- A "suggestion box" in the front office and at a link on our Web site. Please share your thoughts with us frequently; if you leave us your name and contact information, we will personally respond.

Also, we believe in partnering with families if a student is struggling in learning; please share concerns with the classroom teacher so that you can together discuss intervention planning for home and school. Similarly, your student's teacher will be teaming with you if he or she sees that your child is struggling.

We welcome you to the _____ (year) school year at _____ (school). We hope to see and hear from you often. Please return the bottom portion of this letter with any comments or questions. Please feel free to call or visit our school at any time.

Sincerely,

Principal (Contact Information _____)

FAMILY COMMENTS OR QUESTIONS

Please share any comments or questions with us by returning this portion of the letter to the school with your ideas or feel free to call, e-mail, or communicate in a way that works for you.

Source: Adapted from Colorado Department of Education, *Family and community partnering: "On the team and at the table,"* Author, Denver, CO, 2009.

Tool 3.2

Family-School Partnering (FSP)

Teacher Two-Way Welcome Letter

Date _____

Dear Families,

Welcometothenewschoolyearat_____(school).
I am looking forward to getting to know you and your student
this year. I wanted to take this opportunity to share some
information about my class and encourage you to communicate with me.

I am committed to helping every student learn in my class.
I believe it is important for families and schools to partner and
share responsibility for student success. I value family members' expertise about their children. Families know a student
best, and I can learn from you. Also, it is important for the students to know that teachers and families are working together
to support their learning. Specifically, I want to share more
about class communication, expectations, and events for the
upcoming year. More specific information from your students
will be coming your way in the next few weeks.

COMMUNICATION (INCLUDE OWN INFORMATION; ASK FAMILIES TO SHARE)

- I believe in having two-way ongoing communication with
  families. I will be (calling, e-mailing) each of you during the first month; please let me hear from you at any
  time.

CLASS PROCEDURES, SUPPORTS, HOMEWORK (INCLUDE OWN INFORMATION; ASK FAMILIES WHAT THEY NEED)

- Information on our class procedures and positive support system will be coming home with your student the
  first day of school so that you and your student can discuss how we celebrate successes and solve problems.
- Homework helps students to practice what they are learning. It also helps families to understand their student's
  school life. (You can _____.). If ever there is confusion, questions, or concerns about homework, please let
  me know. I will also let you know if I am worried about your
  student's homework completion.

EVENTS (INCLUDE OWN EVENTS; ASK FAMILIES WHAT THEY WOULD LIKE)

Thank you for partnering with me this year concerning your student's success. I look forward to hearing from you. Please return the form below with your comments and contact information, e-mail me at _____, or leave a message at _____ .

Sincerely,

_____

FAMILY COMMENTS OR QUESTIONS

Name: _____

YOUR PREFERRED CONTACT (E-MAIL, MAIL, NOTE WITH STUDENT, TELEPHONE) AND BEST TIMES TO REACH YOU: _____

Source: Adapted from Colorado Department of Education, *Family and community partnering: "On the team and at the table,"* Author, Denver, CO, 2009.

Tool 3.3

Family-School Partnering (FSP)

Family Sharing Sheet

I like to partner with all of my student's families in support-ing their school success. In teaming, it is helpful for me to know about the needs of your student and family and your views about school. Please complete this sheet and return it to me. It may be better for you and your student to com-plete this together. Your individual comments can be put in the labeled boxes. I look forward to partnering with you this year. I want you to feel free to contact me at any time: __ (name and contact information)

My Student Is: _____ I Am: _____

Date: _____

1. My student likes _____ about school.
2. My student has the following strengths in school: _____
   _____.
3. My student's challenges in school are _____
   _____.
4. What are some of your student's interests, activities, and talents?
5. What are some of your interests, activities, and talents that you would be willing to share with the class?

STUDENT COMMENTS:

What else would you like me to know about you this year?

What suggestions do you have for our class?

Other thoughts?

FAMILY COMMENTS:

What else would you like me to know about you
   or your student?
Please share your hopes and dreams for your stu-
   dent's school year.
What are the best ways and times to contact you?
Other thoughts?

Source: Adapted from Colorado Department of Education,
*Family and community partnering: "On the team and at the
table,"* Author, Denver, CO, 2009.

Tool 3.4

Family-School Partnering (FSP)

Guest Response Card

Date:

Directions: Please let us know how we are doing by checking yes or no and leaving this form in the guest response box in the front office.

Date of your visit:	**Yes**	**No**

1. Did you find or get what you were looking for?
2. Were you treated respectfully?
3. Did our staff help you?
4. Did you get the information you requested or needed?
5. Did you feel welcomed?

Please add comments or suggestions for how we can make your visits more positive.

Tool 3.5

Family-School Partnering (FSP)

School Success Pledge

Our school is committed to teachers, students, and families all partnering together for student school success. We would like every teacher, student, and a family member to sign an agreement that says that they will work as a team to support student learning at school and home. This pledge will be reviewed and discussed several times during the school year. Please call _____ with any questions, ideas, or input about this pledge or if you would like to meet personally. We welcome your feedback.

TEACHER PLEDGE

- ✓ I will encourage all students to do their best and to engage in learning every day.
- ✓ I will frequently ask students to discuss school and homework with their families.
- ✓ I will help students and families to understand the class and homework responsibilities.
- ✓ I will welcome student and family input, questions, and ideas throughout the year.
- ✓ Other (Optional): _____
_____

Signature(s): _____ Date(s): _____
Signature(s): _____ Date(s): _____

FAMILY PLEDGE

- ✓ I will encourage my student to do his or her best to work hard and learn every day.
- ✓ I will frequently discuss homework, school learning activities, and the importance of education.

✓ I will provide time, space, and support for homework on a daily basis. This may not be at our home or with me but will be in our community or with family.
✓ I will share my input, questions, and ideas with the teacher throughout the year.
✓ Other (Optional): _____

_____

Signature(s): _____   Date(s): _____
Signature(s): _____   Date(s): _____

STUDENT PLEDGE

✓ I will do my best in school and learning every day.
✓ I will frequently discuss schoolwork and learning activities with my family.
✓ I will complete homework and share what I am learning with my family.
✓ I will ask my teacher or family when I need help or have questions or problems.
✓ Other (Optional):

_____

Signature(s): _____   Date(s): _____
Source: Adapted from Colorado Department of Education, *Family and community partnering: "On the team and at the table,"* Author, Denver, CO, 2009.

Tool 3.6

Family-School Partnering (FSP)

Good News Two-Way Postcard

Good News!

Schools, families, and students partnering for school success!

Date:
It makes me proud to tell you that your student accomplished...

_____

_____

_____

Sincerely,
Let us know what you think: _____

_____

Please share some news about your child and return this card to us:

_____

_____

Source: Adapted from Meadow Point Elementary, Aurora Colorado, 2009.

Tool 3.7

Family-School Partnering (FSP)

Two-Way Homework

TWO-WAY COMMUNICATION

Definition: Information about student learning is shared equally between home and school. Schools share with families, and families share with schools.

HOMEWORK

Definition: Tasks are assigned for "out-of-school" time to expand, reinforce, and coordinate learning. Homework is the key everyday connection between home and school. Homework completion is a measure of engaged learning, a component of student school success.

- At the beginning of the term, "assign" students to discuss the homework process with family members and request written, e-mail, or verbal confirmation or feedback from family members; follow up personally if you do not hear back.
- Share homework information with families in multiple venues, such as Web site, e-mails, notes home, handbooks, and phone calls.
- In your homework description, explain the following: your commitment to every student's success; specific homework philosophy and purpose; explicit teacher, student, family responsibilities; time expectations and any individualized procedures; expectation of early family-school two-way communication if problems occur; explanation of shared problem-solving process to resolve concerns.
- Emphasize the importance of families supporting learning at home, every day; discussing school learning, encouraging efforts, and providing time for homework are easily implemented and effective home practices.
- Include a family comment component in homework assignments so that home sharing is invited; students can see the family-school partnering in action; respond to family feedback.

- Develop "interactive homework" assignments in which students and families work together in learning; this can be students teaching families or shared activities; inform families; do regularly; require family feedback for each assignment; share that you do not expect perfection; proactively problem solve for barriers such as illiteracy or language differences.
- Provide easily accessed, individualized "homework help" for students or families when either might be struggling independently or together; include models and examples. It is all about student success.
- Keep data on homework completion; respond regularly and proactively to students and families; jointly celebrate successes and address concerns.

Source: Adapted from Colorado Department of Education, *Family and community partnering: "On the team and at the table,"* Author, Denver, CO, 2009.

Four

Adapting Targeted-Intensive FSP Processes and Practices

> The goal is that educators, family members, and community resources are on the team and at the table in supporting every student's school success.

Colorado Department of Education, 2009

Chapter 4 describes the application of the core universal processes and practices to the targeted-intensive tiers of family-school partnering (FSP). *Teaming interventions* is added as an upper-tier process applied to established practices such as counseling, remedial reading, response-to-intervention (RtI), and special education.

After reviewing this chapter, the reader will

- Apply universal FSP processes and practices to targeted-intensive situations
- Clarify FSP responsibilities and practices in teaming interventions
- Identify specific family-school eliminate interventions

In FSP, the targeted-intensive tiers include all the components established in the foundation and universal tier. These serve as anchors for families and schools to partner more specifically as needed. The clear expectation is that 1–15% of all students, families, and staff may need more targeted-intensive partnering opportunities, and that mechanisms to provide these supports will have been created. In this book, the two upper tiers are discussed together, titled the targeted-intensive tiers or Tiers 2 and 3. These two upper tiers are seen as fluid with a permeable boundary as the needs of students, families, and staff fluctuate in intensity. Upper-tier partnering is on a practice continuum, ranging from informal actions such as a family member consulting with the school social worker about parenting skills to a defined formal structure such as RtI or special education.

The shift into the targeted-intensive FSP tiers can occur for several reasons. A student may be at risk either in academic or social-emotional-behavioral learning. Sometimes, families or teachers/school staff are hesitant, uninformed, or experiencing challenges in partnering concerning a student. Families may need support or information in accessing resources such as community agencies or interpreters or parent education. Targeted-intensive partnering can begin with a request from a teacher or other school personnel; from a family member, including the student; or from a community resource as well.

The legal and research rationale at the root of FSP applies to this targeted-intensive work as well as the broader universal context. The importance of coordinated learning becomes even more salient when students are struggling. Often, more practice, repetition, and generalization experiences are necessary. By deliberately and persistently including families in these targeted-intensive situations, with the specific focus on student success, a more timely understanding of the student's needs is obtained.

The core universal processes are all applied to partnering in Tiers 2 and 3 but with changes in degree. The FSP dimensions that shift when accessing upper tiers are time, duration, intensity, and specificity of prescribed partnering opportunities. When students need more support to be successful in school, more people, in addition to the classroom teacher, become a part of a solution-planning and intervening team. Specific expertise is tapped. Sometimes, this may be an educational specialist working with a student and classroom teacher as an informal team or an attendance administrator working with a student and teacher concerning multiple class absences. Other times, it can be a more formal teaming structure, such as in a special education meeting. In FSP, family members become equal team members, supporting a struggling student, bringing their knowledge of their student and his or her learning at home.

Unfortunately, families are not always seen as integral, natural partners in a teaming process, and they have not typically been given specific roles and responsibilities in supporting their student. At times, during instructional consultation, it has been suggested that parents not be directly involved in the teaming process (Rosenfield, 2008). While this may be understood from a teacher's perspective, it can waste valuable time when a school and family could be coordinating efforts and benefiting from each other's knowledge and resources. Working to ensure families are team members is not inventing new teaming structures or systems but simply integrating families and students more explicitly into existing operations. As Peacock and Collett (2010) stated:

> Parents should be viewed as integral to the solution of any school-based problems children may be exhibiting. However, often we look for solutions only within the schools, where teachers and other school personnel often have limited time and resources. Involving parents in the intervention process can increase the opportunities for positive outcomes. (p. 87)

A slide presentation for school staff and families, explaining teaming interventions and upper-tier practices, has been designed for adaptable site use.

Check Out This FSP Tool: *FSP Targeted-Intensive Stakeholder Slides*

CORE UNIVERSAL FSP PROCESSES IN THE TARGETED-INTENSIVE TIERS

The core universal processes—building relationships, creating welcoming settings, using two-way communication, and educating all partners—play a more explicit role in the upper tiers. At the targeted-intensive levels, families and school staff may have already experienced hurdles to successfully partnering concerning a child's school success. Various levels of effectiveness may have been experienced, with relationships becoming burdened by ongoing needs for intervention or support despite months or even years of hard work. To fully and collaboratively partner with families when stress mounts and when people may not have the answers they seek, the most important groundwork to be laid is a basic and fundamental level of trust (Minke, 2008). As a result, the core universal processes must become more individualized, specialized, and unique to specific student, family, and school staff needs. A few representative examples of universal processes applied to the upper-tier situations are described next; there are others, but we felt these were the most common and relevant targeted-intensive issues.

Build Relationships

Time and sensitivity are required in targeted-intensive partnering relationships. Efficacy related to student, teacher, and family members' sense of competence in working with a student's challenges is important to consider (Christenson & Anderson, 2002; Esler et al., 2008; Hoover-Dempsey & Sandler, 1997; Manz, Mautone, & Martin, 2009). A focus on strengths is important, relating to both students and adults. Past conflictual or failure experiences can leave residual feelings that interfere with partnering (Minke, 2008). For teachers, this may include negative interactions with families in the past or personal experiences that interfere with comfortable family communication. For family members, there may be a hesitancy in becoming involved with the school because of their own painful memories or feelings of inadequacy in working with the educational system. Both teachers and families may be uncomfortable or feel inadequate when there are differences such as language, cultures, gender preference, or socioeconomic level (Christenson, 2004). Specific targeted-intensive tier applications in building relationships are described next.

Respond to the Grieving Process

When a child is diagnosed with a disability or a mental illness, a family often experiences stages of grieving and emotional learning (Naseef, 2001). Moses (1983) described this process as the continuous mourning over the loss of a normal child. Depending on age of the child and the family's supports and protective factors, various strategies may be helpful at specific times. In partnering at the targeted-intensive tiers, it is important that school staff be aware of the possible grieving stages and incorporate that knowledge into the partnering processes. Kubler-Ross (1969), in her original work on death and dying, identified the stages as denial, anger, depression, bargaining, and acceptance. Naseef (2001) described how families may continually reexperience these feelings, challenging school and community staff to understand and support as needed. He described the family-professional interactions as "perilous partnerships." Moses (1983) talked about the importance of supporting the family in accepting a new and different reality. He offered these words to guide professionals:

> How do parents survive the loss of a profound and central dream shattered by an impairment? How do parents grow from such a trauma and become enhancers of their child's life as well as of their own lives? The answer appears to lie in working through grief in the context of meaningful human relationships. A meaningful relationship is defined as one that gives a bereaved person the human environment in which to feel and share the potent emotions of grief. (p. 16)

Similarly, because there can be a genetic component in some diagnosed conditions, families themselves may be struggling with challenges similar to those of the student.

Develop Individual Relationships

Reaching out personally to staff or families who are hesitant to become involved in FSP is sometimes an action implemented by a specialist such as a school mental health professional. Building trusting relationships can be difficult because of emotional risk and lack of dedicated time (Minke, 2008). Uncomfortable staff or families usually have specific reasons for their hesitancy, and these need to be explored in a sensitive manner. Asking for input and respecting opinions are helpful in both understanding the situation and addressing identified issues (Sheridan et al., 2008). Developing personal relationships over time, persistently encouraging participation, demonstrating genuine empathy, and providing information are all recommended. Keeping conversations focused on student school success reduces defensiveness and distance (Christenson & Sheridan, 2001). Emphasizing the educational importance of FSP related to learning (Christenson, 2004), including training and support if needed, highlights the rationale and can invite new thinking about FSP. "Never giving up" is an important belief in individual family outreach, paired with the understanding that time and patience are required. Sometimes, daily caring communication is the consistent messaging that needs to occur in convincing families of genuine outreach and desire to partner.

Create Welcoming Settings

At the targeted-intensive levels, the intention to create an environment conducive to partnering continues to be an important way to set the stage for effective family-school relationships, just as in the universal tier. Because some of the interactions in these tiers may have tenors of stress simply because the student's needs are intensifying, anything that can contribute to a supportive, collaborative setting can help facilitate positive family-school partnerships.

Design Comfortable Venues

Home visits, sharing coffee, small meetings, and cozy venues should all be considered. Serving food and including the families in choosing times and locations for meetings can give a respectful and important message about their importance as full partners. Including collaborative efforts in planning with home and school participants is helpful and involves such gestures as asking the family what might be helpful to them (Minke & Anderson, 2008). Smaller meetings, with only those staff truly needing to be present, often create a more comfortable and efficient setting for all meeting attendees (S. Kraft, personal communication, May 22, 2009). Similarly, communicating in an ongoing way with casual conversations between dyads and triads is often more efficient than formal meetings for all stakeholders. Sometimes, it just needs to be a "chat."

Instill a Responsive Atmosphere

Facilitation of meetings and interactive discussions needs to be thoughtful and intentional at the targeted-intensive tiers (Minke & Anderson, 2008). Preparation, organization, and knowing participants' purposes are all important in effective discussions. In FSP, it is suggested that a liaison be identified at the school when a family is addressing upper-tier issues (Colorado Department of Education, 2008a; Miller & Kraft, 2008). For both professionals and families, this person can be available for questions about team processes and support true teaming. The central role of identifying strengths, both for a student and a family, in Tiers 2 and 3, helps the family to feel respected and included (Miller & Kraft, 2008; Sheridan et al., 2008). Minke and Anderson (2008) stressed that relatively minor events can develop meaningful participation of families. These can include ensuring that families have time on the agenda, asking family members to bring their data, ensuring that students are present and participatory, providing information in advance, and supporting co-facilitation between family members and professionals.

Use Two-Way Communication

Communication in the upper tiers often needs to be more intentional and frequent than in Tier 1 (Colorado Department of Education, 2008b). Issues are more serious, and student school success is at risk. An explicit plan is usually developed as part of intervention teaming, and there must be clear, coordinated expectations for home and school. The student often adopts a specific role in the plan, and it is important for him or her to understand the partnering communication for his or her success. Various venues to communicate should be explored with all partners so that those chosen can be efficient and effective. Suggestions might be the use of e-mail, telephone, before or afterschool face-to-face conversations, text messaging, back-and-forth books, or regular meetings. The key is for all communication to be specific, two way, and agreed on by home and school. Specific targeted-intensive tier applications in two-way communication are described next.

Resolve Conflicts

A process for identifying and resolving conflict is needed in the teaming process. Sometimes conflict, misunderstandings, and communication breakdowns occur between home and school. In FSP, however, there is a commitment to resolve differences in the best interest of the student and his or her school success. The recognition of such a possibility should be accepted and resources allocated as needed. It is important that there be a process to resolve concerns in a positive manner. School mental health professionals and administrators can be available to work with parties and problem solve when conflicts arise between families and staff members.

Conflict occurs when families and school staff are working together to support students because there are differing viewpoints, philosophies, and goals. Discussing and respecting differences can ignite helpful changes in practice and force courageous conversations (Minke & Anderson, 2008). A common dynamic, however, is that families are usually focusing only on their student, whereas school educators are working with many students. Conflict can be more common and more intense when a student is struggling since issues of efficacy, frustration, and discouragement emerge on all sides. If a solid, tiered FSP framework is in place, it is hoped that destructive conflict can be minimized if from the beginning there has been a goal of working together for the student and of creating trusting relationships between all partners.

Differences that occur when families and schools partner should be accepted respectfully with an eye toward compromise and mutually acceptable solutions. Simple strategies in a meeting include "check-ins" to assess how participants are feeling when disagreement occurs and beginning a meeting by framing conflict as a possible occurrence so that it is viewed as something that can be expressed and overcome. The use of objective data and jointly developed measurable goals also helps keep a conflict focused on solving a student issue and mutually obtained information. Christenson and Sheridan (2001) outlined effective strategies and communication skills that can resolve a specific concern and maintain respectful relationships. They suggested separating the person from the issue, focusing on mutual interests, exploring several options, and basing decisions on objective criteria. Helpful communication skills for resolving conflict are active listening, paraphrasing, humor, and summarizing. Sometimes, conflict resolution requires mediation or legal action, such as is formally available in special education (Wright & Wright, 2005). With genuine and ongoing partnering practices, the hope is that these formal processes would be needed minimally as they can be time consuming, expensive, and draw resources away from student instructional time.

Stabilize Crises

A second communication skill that is required as a part of targeted-intensive teaming is how to help stabilize a student, family, or staff member during an unsettling, difficult experience or crisis. It is crucial for some students or families experiencing significant concerns to access support during a crisis as optimal school performance depends on physical, cognitive, and emotional availability (Brock, 2002). FSP is the core of effective crisis intervention, with schools and families working together to create multisystem supports. The school mental health professional or other staff might be called in to offer interventions. This could include stabilization and contact with outside mental health workers when someone is considering committing suicide, family contact to calm a highly anxious or disruptive child, or problem solving with a concerned staff member. Crisis intervention frequently includes teaming interventions and home-school-home monitoring (Brock, 2002). There is a significant need for two-way (or "multiple-way") communication to successfully plan and link family-school-community support.

Educate Partners

Mutual education is especially critical at the targeted-intensive tiers; there may be multiple team members with diverse skills and different levels of familiarity with the identified issues. Providing all team members with specific knowledge of procedural steps and data use will make meetings effective and efficient. This includes families and community resources in addition to school staff. Classroom teachers may not be familiar with how to partner directly with specialists to develop shared interventions and monitor progress. Administrators may benefit from understanding how to invite families to help find solutions when behavior problems arise as they are often accustomed to managing such issues independently. There needs to be an established norm that "none of us have all the answers" and "we are all learning with each other." Specific Tier 2 and Tier 3 skills in educating partners are described next.

Link Families With Community Resources

Connecting families with community resources is often a practice that occurs as a result of ongoing interventions at school when there is the realization that supplementary support is indicated or because of a family request. School personnel who work with families in the upper tiers should be knowledgeable about availability, accessibility, and appropriateness of resources for specific needs (Eagle, Dowd-Eagle, & Sheridan, 2008). Empowering families to independently identify areas of strengths, concerns, and support occurs within the context of family-centered practices during collaboration with a school professional (Sheridan et al., 2008). It is helpful to have an established protocol that includes a discussion of financial and insurance issues, collaborative partnering with the school, and ongoing follow-up support for the family. "Family-driven care" (Duchnowski & Kutash, 2007) stresses the importance of the family seeing the school and community supports as a continuum or "system of care." This requires joint education about how each system operates so that each partner understands his or her shared role in supporting a student or family.

Develop Targeted Skills

Providing information or education to school staff, community resources, or families plays an important role in upper-tier FSP, although the venue may not always be the educational setting. Often, the focus is on how to reinforce or increase adult skills and confidence needed to support student success. For any stakeholder, this may take the form of teaching a specific skill, informing about a diagnosed condition, or learning how to engage in a specific legal, educational, or therapeutic process.

For families, education may involve counseling concerning a child's specific disability, which is an available related service for family members (U.S. Department of Education, 2006). There are also various formats and evidence-based programs for family education that focus on parenting skills, family functioning, and supporting learning at home. The Future of School Psychology Task Force on Family-School

Partnerships (2007) defined *parent education* as "a systematic presentation of information to parents for the purpose of supporting their efforts and abilities to promote their child's development" (Module 4). *Family support* is a newer term, implying a more equal power differential. Parent education might be offered to a wide audience or small group to teach or practice general concepts. A more intensive educative experience is *family intervention* or *family therapy*, which focuses on "a systematic therapeutic process with parents (and other family members) that focuses on interpersonal relationships and effective child management strategies for the purpose of modifying identified sources of child distress" (Future of School Psychology Task Force, 2007, Module 4). This last experience would most often be offered to the family in the community, with school collaboration concerning the student's school success.

THE TARGETED-INTENSIVE FSP PROCESS: TEAM INTERVENTIONS

An additional FSP process that is required as a part of the targeted-intensive tiers *team interventions*. The definition of *teamwork* is "work done by several associates with each doing a part, but all subordinating personal prominence to the efficiency of the whole" (Merriam-Webster, 2004). Student interventions at school are defined as a set of actions, focused on academic or social-emotional-behavioral concerns that are "designed to help a student improve performance relative to a specific, realistic, and measurable goal. Interventions are based on valid information about current performance and are realistic for implementation" (Cherry Creek Schools, 2006, p. 14).

Teams and support services designed to address student concerns are common in schools. Teams tend to be composed primarily of building staff members who meet regularly to discuss students and brainstorm suggestions. These teams have been called teacher assistance teams (Chalfant, Pysh, & Moultrie, 1979) or instructional consultation teams (Rosenfield, 2008). Related are special education multidisciplinary teams that follow mandated procedures. Unfortunately, these various school teaming practices do not always include family members and students as equal team members who are invited from the beginning to be at meetings to share in assessing, planning, and intervening. In some circumstances, families have to give consent and be invited, such as in special education, but in other cases they may not be informed of focused conversation or meetings about their student. Support services are generally provided by school specialists, often with "parent consent" or knowledge, but rarely with explicit FSP to coordinate learning, support generalization of new skills, and help in assessing progress.

Research investigating the barriers to collaborating with families in intervention planning suggested that it is most frequently the attitudes and behaviors of the school-based professionals that control the level of parental participation (Christenson & Sheridan, 2001; Dauber & Epstein, 1993). Teams do not always provide opportunities for parents to collaborate in decision making or in intervention implementation, despite the fact that most parents want to be involved in their child's education (Christenson, 2004; Harry, 1992).

In FSP, interventions for students at the targeted-intensive tiers are prescribed, implemented, and monitored by families and educators working together as a team. There must be a shift in practice to include the family members in discussions about their student. This participation is especially important in early stages when a school staff member indicates concern about a student's success so that family information and expertise can be included in the conversation. This inclusion must be genuine, truly participatory, and expected by all stakeholders. FSP teaming needs to become the way it is always done. In referring to this upper-tier FSP process, the Colorado Department of Education (2009) used the words "On the Team and At the Table" (p. 7) as described in Table 4.1.

Implement Teaming Four Steps

Teaming interventions for student school success is best implemented within a basic four-step, problem-solving model, which includes data collection, goal setting, progress monitoring, and evaluation. The four steps are *define, plan, implement,* and *evaluate.* They are described in Table 4.2 and elaborated in Chapter 5. This basic process is also typically seen in RtI and behavioral models. Approaches that follow this basic process have resulted in improved outcomes for students (Kovaleski, Gickling, Morrow, & Swank, 1999). Family members and students should explicitly be on the team and at the table with school staff through these steps. There is mutual accountability for implementation and decisions. There must be a focus on measurable results, implementing plans as intended, and ongoing responsiveness to data. By consistently using data to

Table 4.1   Family and Community Partnering: "On the Team and at the Table"

"On the Team"

On a football team, every player has a job to do and a role to play. Each player is respected for his or her unique expertise. Each player practices and works to become better at executing personal responsibilities. The team works together to obtain the best results possible.

"At the Table"

Picture a table where people are discussing an issue. Every involved party has a place at the table, even though he or she might not be present. All listen and respect each other's ideas. There is disagreement at times, but intentional effort is made to understand differences and compromise for positive outcomes. All voices are heard.

(*Source:* Colorado Department of Education, *Family and community partnering: "On the team and at the table,"* Author, Denver, CO, 2009.)

Table 4.2   Family-School Partnering (FSP): Teaming Four Steps

Applications: Academic and social-emotional-behavioral interventions, response-to-intervention (RtI), special education, school-home-school notes, conjoint behavioral consultation (CBC), and wraparound

1. Define
- Collect and review data
- Map strengths and resources
- Identify hurdles

2. Plan
- Prioritize measurable goals
- Identify actions and interventions
- Assign responsibilities, resources, and timelines
- Choose measurement tools

3. Implement
- Follow plan as intended
- Monitor progress

4. Evaluate
- Assess goal attainment and implementation
- Revise plan
- Continue

Note: Individual step terminology and order may vary slightly in different applications, programs, structures, and sites. These are also the basic action-planning cycle steps depicted in Chapter 5.

assess effectiveness, objective decisions can be made about student school success versus decisions based only on perceptions, beliefs, and assumptions.

While some problem-solving processes may have their own terminology and procedural requirements, they have these same core sequential actions. However, basic similarities are often not perceived by staff and families across the many different teams seen in schools, including special education. Thus, if all teamed interventions can use a similar framework and terminology for an ongoing, data-driven, results-focused, and collaborative process, there will be greater understanding across teams. Once specific terminology and procedures are mastered, they can be applied and generalized by all stakeholders across many situations. As part of any school teaming process, it is important to have "family-friendly" letters, forms, and information to explain how and why families are invited to the table as full team members and what they might expect during their team participation. There are two dimensions integral to implementing the four steps of teaming interventions: clarifying roles and responsibilities and using shared data. Each of these dimensions is discussed in more detail in the following sections with accompanying FSP tools linked to identified actions.

Check Out These FSP Tool: *FSP Teaming Invitation, FSP Teaming Interventions: What Families Need to Know, FSP Teaming Questions for Families and Educators to Ask Together*

Clarify Roles and Responsibilities

Directly encouraging and supporting a family member's participation in teaming interventions is important as this is most likely a new experience. Specifically, his or her ongoing role in teaming interventions will need to be defined and guided (Miller & Kraft, 2008). Similarly, classroom teachers and other team members may not have worked directly with families in such a defined, continuous process. Collaborating as partners in examining data, developing and implementing interventions, monitoring progress, and evaluating effectiveness are often new skills for all participants. Clear communication, common language, and identified role expectations are important in creating successful team partnering. Much of intervention teaming can occur outside formal meetings through informal communication and data sharing. Maintaining a focus on the student and the student's progress is helpful for both teachers and families in overcoming interpersonal hesitancy.

Family-centered approaches (Dunst et al., 1994; Sheridan et al., 2008) and family-driven care (Duchnowski & Kutash, 2007) have identified key elements that empower families to share in their student's support and decision making as members of the team. The following components are recommended for any team process: respond to child- and family-identified needs, promote child and family strengths, use effective help-giving practices such as encouraging competence and independence, and identify support networks (Sheridan et al., 2008).

We would argue that upper-tier teams or support services cannot be totally school-centric, family-centric, or community-centric but must orchestrate all these partners to be *student-centric*. This means empowering all to participate fully in ensuring that student success is the primary agenda item at all times. Each partner brings unique expertise and strengths that must be valued in the team process. Such recognition empowers each partner to fulfill his or her role to increase effective participation in a specific student-focused intervention. Table 4.3 describes specific roles and responsibilities, helping provide common understanding for all partners.

Use Shared Data

The four steps of teaming interventions are driven by data. In FSP, the data are shared among team members, including families. The amount, frequency, and nature of data collected and monitored in teaming interventions are directly related to the intensity of student and family need (Colorado Department of Education, 2008b; National Association of Special Education Directors, 2006). Data are collected from multiple sources, including school staff, students, and family members. Different types of data, both existing and collected, are included to plan, implement, and monitor interventions. Examination of visual data is one way partners can experience a shared understanding of the student's strengths, progress, and concerns (Miller & Kraft, 2008). Family, students, and school staff partner in determining needs for additional data and work together to obtain this information. When data points are shared between

Table 4.3 Family-School Partnering (FSP): Roles and
Responsibilities in Teaming Interventions

Applications: Academic and social-emotional-behavioral interventions, response-to-intervention (RtI), special education, school-home-school notes, conjoint behavioral consultation (CBC), and wraparound

School Roles and Responsibilities

- Always partner initially with families at the universal, classroom level so that concerns and home-school strategies are discussed openly.
- Provide clear, understandable information on the specific teaming process.
- Personally invite families to attend all intervention team meetings as equal members; develop alternative ways to include families in the teaming if they cannot attend the discussion.
- Create a structure for genuine family sharing, planning participation, and intervention implementation; teaming interventions often happens outside meetings through progress monitoring and informal communication.
- Include students whenever appropriate.
- Tell the student that the school and his or her family are working together to support his or her school success.
- Assign a staff liaison to support families in the teaming process; this person can answer questions, encourage participation, communicate or coach about interventions.
- Provide information on how to support the targeted skill learning at home.
- Give copies of intervention plans, curricula highlights, and progress-monitoring data to families.

Family Roles and Responsibilities

- Work with your student's classroom teacher to discuss concerns and develop support strategies for home and school.
- Review provided information on specific teaming process for your student.
- Attend school workshops or trainings related to teaming interventions.
- Observe and ask your student about school learning and experiences.
- Attend the team meetings when there is planning for your student's interventions; if you cannot attend, ask about other ways to participate, such as conference calls, taped meetings, e-mails, home visits, or out-of-school meetings.
- Share relevant information about your student, especially regarding his or her strengths, challenges, attitude about school, school history, and homework habits.
- Tell your student that you are working with the school to help him or her succeed.
- Know a school staff member you can ask about your partnering role or your student's intervention plan.
- Ask how you can support your student's targeted skill learning at home.

partners, they become more relevant and meaningful measures of a student's school success.

A specific data source in teaming interventions is diagnostic/prescriptive assessment. The major purpose of such assessments is to provide "information for planning more effective instruction and intervention" (Colorado Department of Education, 2008a, p. 30). Diagnostic/prescriptive assessment should be available as needed, not just as a component of the special education process. During FSP, families, including students, participate actively in any diagnostic/prescriptive assessment decisions. They must be thoroughly informed regarding the explicit purpose, conditions, results, and practical application related to any recommended assessment. This occurs naturally if families and students are teaming around intervention planning and implementation. Any assessment should honor a student's time and be tied to a clearly articulated question related to school success (Brown-Chidsey, 2005). Threat or suicide evaluations are included as they inform adult and student action planning; families are included as key informants.

A tradition of administering a battery of tests for learning or emotional concerns has developed in many schools, especially related to special education eligibility. This practice sometimes results in a blanket-type permission for the school to administer a variety of assessments, which are often not clearly explained to families. Families are then given the results in a combined format, framed under such terms as "special education eligibility" or "comprehensive assessment," which can result in confusion about what the findings mean regarding improving school success. The Final Rule for Individuals With Disabilities Education Improvement Act 2004 (U.S. Department of Education, 2006) states that parents must be participants in reviewing existing data to determine "what, if any, additional data is needed," and this review must include "evaluations and information from the parent" (p. 46785). These regulations are intended to ensure that families are involved in the decision making about needed assessments in special education. In a similar vein, Sheridan and McCurdy (2005) discussed the importance of including ecological factors in any assessment, implying the inclusion of families in the evaluation of important contextual home variables. Families are often the only partners in teaming interventions who have the longitudinal perspective, and their information enriches all diagnostic/prescriptive data.

Check Out These FSP Tools: *FSP Team Family Information, FSP Team Intervention Plan With Strengths and Family Coordination, FSP Permission for Diagnostic/Prescriptive Assessment*

Teaming Interventions for Individuals, Small Groups, and Established Structures

Team interventions for student concerns can be provided individually or for small groups of students and can be a component of set structures such as RtI or special education. They can also be provided within a federal program or a continuum of services in a specific district. Interventions are provided for a wide variety of issues, such as poor reading comprehension, writing deficiencies, truancy, anger management concerns, or bullying. One type of group intervention becoming more common is the standard treatment protocol, defined as "a set of evidence-based practices provided to those students who display predictable difficulties. These interventions are designed to be used in a systematic manner with all participating students. … Student progress is monitored frequently and instruction is fine-tuned based on student response" (National Association of State Directors of Special Education, 2006, p. 24). However, in most cases, there has been no mention of how families might be included in such standard protocols.

In our FSP framework, both individual and group interventions include families as essential partners because of the importance of coordinated learning and the effectiveness of positive, informed home support (Miller & Kraft, 2008). Interventions either can have defined, specific roles and training for families, such as in parent tutoring, or can prescribe general support activities. The level of family participation may vary from specific, daily assigned practice and data collection to informal student conversation. In all cases, however, families are informed and teaming in the intervention. Specific suggestions for several types of teaming interventions and delivery structures are outlined next.

Social-Emotional-Behavioral and Academic Interventions

Social skill development, anger control, stress and anxiety management, family change adjustment, and school success skills can all be a focus of school-based social-emotional-behavioral interventions, such as in counseling or support groups (Peacock & Collett, 2010). Families and classroom teachers alike are seen as partnering in assessment, reinforcement, and practice of a student's social-emotional-behavioral learning. Specific FSP activities may be prescribed by a program or theoretical orientation. In general, there seems to be wide-spread agreement among mental health practitioners regarding the effectiveness and importance of family participation in children's or adolescents' treatment and social-emotional-behavioral learning (Corey & Corey, 2006; Dupaul, Stoner, & O'Reilly, 2008; Friedberg & McClure, 2002; Gilman & Chard, 2007; Gunn, Haley, & Lyness, 2007; Laugeson, Frankel, Mogil, & Dillon, 2009; Prout & Brown, 2007). School mental health practitioners need to be intentional, thoughtful, and persistent about including families in the implementation of social-emotional-behavioral interventions. Individual and group school counseling initiatives should always include "partnering plans" for generalization and continuous growth.

Academic interventions often focus on specific skill sets based on screening results or diagnostic/prescriptive assessment. Family support may be seen in drill practices, review, or specific monitoring. Specificity usually depends on the level of skill required and the family comfort. Peacock and Collett (2010) and the Future of School Psychology Task Force (2007, Module 5) cite numerous academic areas in which family skill reinforcement is effective and easily implemented. These include reading, writing, and math techniques.

Response-to-Intervention (RtI)

FSP practices are also critical when interventions are prescribed for students within an RtI structure. RtI is a relatively new tiered instructional teaming approach for all students but with a focus on students who are struggling in school. RtI models usually include a team problem-solving process that examines student data, prescribes research-based interventions, measures intervention effectiveness, and adapts strategies accordingly. In most RtI frameworks, referrals can originate with teachers or families or from universal screening results. Information from RtI is one allowed criterion in IDEA 2004 (U.S. Department of Education, 2006) for identifying students with specific learning disabilities. If a school is using RtI in this way, all partners should be aware of this special education possibility when it is first initiated with a student. In an RTI model, as in any shared endeavor, it is important that staff and families have a common understanding of the terms, core components, and responsibilities.

Currently, RTI in FSP may look different from school to school, depending on such factors as age of students, community characteristics, state/district requirements, and staff-family training. FSP in RtI has been explicitly recommended by various researchers and organizations (Burns & Gibbons, 2008; Burns, Wiley, & Viglietta, 2008; Reschly, Coolong-Chaffin, Christenson, & Gutkin 2007; Wright, 2007). Some states explicitly include families throughout the process (Callendar, 2007; Colorado Department of Education, 2008b; Graden, Stollar, & Poth, 2007; Peterson, Prasse, Shinn, & Swerdlik, 2007).

Special Education

Similar to RtI, FSP is essential for interventions that are prescribed for students who have been identified as having disabilities. Special education is an important, school-based legal process with numerous mandates and specified parameters. Unfortunately, as found by the President's Commission on Excellence in Special Education (2002), this process has become overly focused on procedures and paperwork to the neglect of student outcomes. In our experience, family participation is dictated by due process rights and seldom includes active teaming in regard to assessment, coordinated intervention planning and implementation, and progress monitoring. Even after a child is identified as having a disability, families may not understand the specific learning or emotional concerns or why certain interventions have been adopted (Peacock & Collett, 2010).

Harry (1992) specifically addressed the common role of the special education parent as only a "consent giver" by recommending that parents become coassessors and coteachers in the special education process. Naseef (2001) stated that, in reality, many family members of children with disabilities are already intimately involved with assessing, teaching, and partnering with professionals regarding their children's progress, outside the special education process. Herr and Bateman (2006) provided explicit guidance on improving the special education Individualized Educational Plan (IEP) process by including parents as authentic participants and focusing on obtaining baselines, prioritizing measurable goals, and assessing progress objectively. They stressed the importance of clarity and a results focus, using data. It was their belief that one of the most prevalent causes of special education due process hearings and adversarial actions between families and schools is the lack of mutually developed measurable goals and regularly shared objective data in measuring progress toward these goals.

Our recommendation is that special education, from eligibility assessment to IEP development to ongoing instruction, be viewed as a teamed intervention with ongoing family partnering at all junctures. The same basic principles as seen in jointly planning any intervention apply: focusing on student success, using ongoing shared data collection in decision making, using the four teaming steps, and including students and families as equal team members in supporting learning at home and school. By reframing special education as a teamed intervention, the spirit of IDEA 2004 can become reality: ongoing school success for students with disabilities. Specific FSP special education ideas are provided in Table 4.4.

Teaming Interventions With Family-School Protocols

The home-school connection can be the primary framework in teaming and be implemented as the intervention itself (Peacock & Collett, 2010), or it can be a model for sharing responsibilities between families and staff. Targeted plans, explicitly developed by families and school staff, with carefully scripted responsibilities have been effective for increasing prosocial skills, decreasing problem behaviors, and improving academic performance (Sheridan & Kratochwill, 2008). Usually, these are individual interventions that are monitored and revised according to data obtained at home and school. Specific family-school interventions can potentially be integrated into all teaming intervention practices, such as RtI or special education, with adaptations to match specific goals and as a prescribed intervention.

An example of a family-school protocol is when, at the targeted-intensive tiers, homework completion becomes an area of home-school focus with struggling students. Both academic and social-emotional-behavioral factors may be evident in a homework problem (Peacock & Collett, 2010). School-home communication is vital to homework interventions (Dawson, 2008). School-home-school notes (or home-school-home notes) provide a systematic frame and are similar to a traditional behavioral contracting system but directly link home responses to school behaviors (Jurbergs, Palcic, & Kelly, 2007; Kelly, 1990). The student actively participates in school-home communication, monitoring, and teaming, allowing for coordination of learning between home and school. Formats vary, but a common frame includes the following basic components: identifying target academic skills or behaviors; developing a method to track progress; applying home-based contingencies; employing strengths; establishing clear responsibilities for school staff and family members; and developing a two-way communication system (Future of School Psychology Task Force, on Family School

Table 4.4　Family-School Partnering (FSP): Teaming Interventions in Special Education

Family-school partnering in the special education eligibility and IEP development process supports positive student outcomes and legal mandates (U.S. Department of Education, 2006). A common special education process, as described by Yell and Stecker (2003), is contrasted with special education as an FSP teamed intervention.

Common Special Education Process	FSP Special Education Process
ASSESSMENT AND ELIGIBILITY • Student is assessed through a predetermined battery of standardized instruments to determine eligibility. • Assessment does not necessarily address instructionally relevant needs that might relate to reason for referral, progress in the general education curriculum, or link to interventions.	ASSESSMENT AND ELIGIBILITY • School representative calls or meets with family to review existing data, obtain family input, and jointly decide on an individual assessment plan directly relevant to prescribing interventions and specific disability decision making. • If student has been in the response-to-intervention (RtI) process, there can be continued partnering around progress monitoring to inform assessment and instruction in the special education process.
GOAL SETTING • One or more of the school staff IEP team members selects goals that are transferred from a goal bank. • Goals are often not based on the assessment or measurable enough to determine whether they will be met. • When families arrive at the meeting, the prepared IEP is presented to them with the expectation that they will review and sign.	GOAL SETTING • Before the IEP is developed, the family, as team members, contributes ideas for needed intervention or instruction; then, the team, including family members, prioritizes and finalizes annual measurable goals. • Goals are objective and measurable; they guide everyday instructional intervention at home and school. • There is mutual discussion of how learning can be coordinated between home and school. • If student has been in the RtI process, those intervention goals may be continued in special education.
INTERVENTION AND PROGRESS MONITORING • After the IEP is signed, it is often placed in a filing cabinet until the IEP team meets again in a year. • It does not necessarily inform instruction, is usually not used to monitor progress, and is a compulsory exercise in legal compliance with the law.	INTERVENTION AND PROGRESS MONITORING • Family and school staff together decide on reasonable, time-efficient tools and time frame with which to measure progress, including how existing data collection might be used to guide instruction. • There is mutual discussion about how home monitoring might be included. • If child has been in the RtI process, monitoring may be continued.

Table 4.5   Family-School Partnering (FSP): Sample School-Home-School Note or Home-School-Home Note

Name: PK		Date: 1/6/10			
Home and School Goals	School Period 1	School Period 2	School Period 3	Homework	Other
1. Follow directions first time.	**0 1** 2	**0 1** 2	**0 1** 2	**0 1** 2	**0 1** 2
2. Finish assignments.	**0 1** 2	**0 1** 2	0 **1** 2	0 **1** 2	**0 1** 2
3. Take short breaks when needed.	0 **1** 2	**0 1** 2	0 **1** 2	0 **1** 2	**0 1** 2
Totals					
Teacher Initials	__CL__	__CL__	__CL__		
Family Initials	__MK__	_____			
Student Initials	_PK___	_PK___	_PK___	__PK__	_____

Successes and Comments: PK: I didn't finish my homework or take breaks because I was sick. I did ok in school.

Key
0 = No
1 = Somewhat...
2 = Yes!!

Goal for Today: __75____%
Total for Today: __75____%

Source: Adapted from Colorado Department of Education, *Family and community partnering: "On the team and at the table,"* Author, Denver, CO, 2009.

Partnerships, 2007; Peacock & Collett, 2010). Consultation with someone such as a school mental health professional can help with breakdowns at school, home, or in between until systems are fine-tuned and working (Peacock & Collett, 2010). A completed school-home-school note, showing shared goals at home and school, is displayed in Table 4.5. Two specific family-school protocols, conjoint behavioral consultation (CBC) and wraparound, are summarized next. Each has unique features and roles within the targeted-intensive tiers. CBC is often implemented to support partnering in specific home-school interventions, and wraparound is typically utilized to include a broader community context for more complex issues.

 Check Out This FSP Tool: *FSP School-Home-School Note or Home-School-Home Note*

Conjoint Behavioral Consultation

Conjoint behavioral consultation (CBC) has been defined as "a structured, indirect form of service delivery, in which parents and teachers work together to address the academic, social, or behavioral needs of an individual for whom both parties bear some responsibility" (Sheridan & Kratochwill, 1992, p.122). In CBC, parents, teachers, and other caregivers engage in a structured problem-solving process with a consultant, usually a school mental health professional. The four problem-solving steps are needs identification, needs analysis, plan implementation, and plan evaluation. Sheridan and Kratochwill (2008) have suggested that CBC can bring the family component and levels of intervention training to the RtI problem-solving process. They summarized the research supporting the effectiveness of CBC with various academic and behavioral concerns across age levels.

Wraparound

Wraparound is a family-school protocol that coordinates comprehensive systems of care for students with the most severe and persistent concerns. Families are active, central partners, and community agencies are often involved, utilizing a special format for planning student interventions. Wraparound promotes a philosophical and literal "wrapping of services" by which the whole needs of the student and family are addressed through a strength-based approach to service planning. While many wraparound programs have been community based in the past, advocates for school-based wraparound services argue that there are many benefits for using the school as the entry point for collaborative family-school-community services (Eber, 2003). More specifically, children spend a significant portion of their day in the school context, and school remains the primary setting for the establishment of primary and secondary interventions. Youth who received services under the wraparound model have been found to be more likely to remain in their home school, demonstrate positive classroom performance, and have a reduced number of residential placements (Eber, Rolf, & Schreiber, 1996). Eber (2003) and Eber, Sugai, Smith, and Scott (2002) described specific school applications. Their process has specific steps but follows a basic teaming intervention sequence.

KEY TERMS

- **Conjoint behavioral consultation:** A specific, structured model for developing teacher-family collaboration to address identified student needs; steps are needs identification, needs analysis, plan implementation, and plan evaluation.
- **Interventions:** A set of actions, focused on academic or social-emotional concerns, that are designed to help a student improve relative to a specific goal.
- **Response to intervention (RtI):** A term used to describe multitier, data-driven instructional approaches, which include the use of research-based interventions and usually a team problem-solving process.
- **School-home-school or home-school-home notes:** A system of planning and implementing a school-home contingency system to support academic and social-emotional-behavioral learning with mutual goals and monitoring.
- **Special education:** The legal structure under IDEA 2004 for identifying and serving students with disabilities.
- **Standard treatment protocol interventions:** A set of evidence-based interventions provided to groups of students with similar, predictable identified difficulties.
- **Targeted-intensive tiers:** Tier 2 and Tier 3 of the multitier FSP framework that provide focused and individualized partnering processes and practices for staff, students, and families.
- **Teaming interventions:** The upper-tier process that is defined as school staff and families working as equal team members in prescribing, implementing, and monitoring interventions when a student is struggling; includes implementing four steps, clarifying roles, and sharing data.
- **Wraparound:** A team-based, family-driven approach to coordinating "systems of care" for students with the most persistent and severe concerns.

TOOL DESCRIPTIONS

FSP Targeted-Intensive Stakeholder Slides. These slides present information for families and school staff on the core partnering processes applied at the targeted and intensive tiers; teaming interventions is defined, including clarifying roles, using shared data, and following steps: *define, plan, implement, and evaluate* (CD only).

Following Teaming Steps and Clarifying Roles

FSP Teaming Invitation. This invitation explains an intervention team and invites the family to attend a team meeting as a partner.

FSP Teaming Interventions: What Families Need to Know. Formatted as a possible brochure insert, this is a list of specific information a family should know when teaming interventions with the school.

FSP Teaming Questions for Families and Educators to Ask Together. Providing a list of mutual questions for team members (including families and school staff), this tool helps to ensure that teams address all components of teaming interventions consistently.

Using Shared Data

FSP Team Family Information. This sheet guides families in sharing information with teams to help in decision making.

FSP Team Intervention Plan with Strengths and Family Coordination. A student intervention plan, which includes strengths and family coordination and communication, can be used by teams in home-school implementation.

FSP Permission for Diagnostic/Prescriptive Assessment. When diagnostic/prescriptive intervention is recommended, it is important for families to understand the purpose and potential use of the information that will be obtained.

Teaming Specific FSP Interventions

FSP School-Home-School Note or Home-School-Home Note. This is a sample process and form for two-way teamed interventions developed jointly between teachers, students, and families.

RESOURCES

Web Sites

Center for Appropriate Dispute Resolution in Special Education: http://www.directionservice.org/cadre/index.cfm

Offers resources and information related to collaborative resolution of family disagreements about special education and early intervention, including mediation.

National Center on Response to Intervention: http://www.rti4success.org/index.php?option=com_content&task=blogcategory&id=12&Itemid=65

Serves as a national clearinghouse for research and information on RtI, with a specific section relating to families.

National Dissemination Center for Children With Disabilities: http://www.nichcy.org/Pages/Home.aspx

Offers resources, research on effective educational practices, and legal summaries relating to children with disabilities.

National Research Center on Learning Disabilities: http://www.nrcld.org/topics/parents.html

Specific information for parents on identifying specific learning disabilities within an RtI process; defines terms and explains processes.

RtI Action Network: http://www.rtinetwork.org/Parents-and-Families

Provides information on why and how to include families in the RtI process.

Books

Eber, L. (2003). *The art and science of wraparound.* Bloomington, IN: Forum on Education, Indiana University.

Explains and sequences the wraparound process as it can be applied in the school setting.

Herr, C. M., & Bateman, B. D. (2006). *Writing measurable IEP goals and objectives.* Verona, WI: Attainment.

Focuses on specific language and process in writing helpful goals that can be objectively measured as the key component of successful family participation in special education effectiveness.

Jenkins, T. (2007). *When a child struggles in school.* Charleston, SC: Advantage.

Explains to families how the RtI process focuses on intervention and data versus a battery of assessment measures. Also, discusses the role of students and families in learning.

Naseef, R. A. (2001). *Special children, challenged parents: The struggles and rewards of raising a child with a disability.* Baltimore, MD: Brooks.

Describes the experiences of parenting a child with a disability while offering information and advice to families and professionals.

Peacock, G. G., & Collett, B. R. (2010). *Collaborative home/school interventions: Evidence-based solutions for emotional, behavioral, and academic problems.* New York: Guilford.

Provides specific suggestions for supporting home-school work when students are exhibiting emotional, behavioral, or learning problems. Includes practical forms.

Sheridan, S. M., & Kratochwill, T. R. (2008). *Conjoint behavioral consultation: Promoting family-school connections and interventions.* New York: Springer.

Describes a step-by-step guide to implementing conjoint behavioral consultation in conjunction with theory, research, and practical forms.

Tools 4.1–4.7

Family-School Partnering (FSP)

Teaming Invitation

Dear _____   Date: _____

Our school is committed to supporting student success. If a student experiences difficulty in academics or behavior, it is important for schools and families to work together as a team. You are invited to participate in the planning, implementation, and monitoring of your child's interventions. Your participation as a team member provides essential information about your child and helps coordinate learning between home and school. Thank you for partnering with us. Please communicate with us at any time.

As a follow-up to our previous conversation, we would like to invite you to a team meeting on _____ at _____ in _____. The purpose of this team meeting is to share information about _____and discuss how we can partner with you to provide school and home support. Staff members who work with your child will be at the meeting, as well as others who can help in planning for success. If there is anyone you would specifically like to attend from school or elsewhere, please let us know. If this time will not work for you, we will try to reschedule, or we will find a time to share information so that we have your input and ideas. Please let us know what is best for you.

Attached is a family information form. This information can help the school staff to learn more about how you see your child. We will be contacting you before the meeting to review this information with you and answer any questions you may have about this team partnering process.

Sincerely,
Position: _____   Phone: _____
E-mail: _____

Source: Adapted from Cherry Creek Schools, *Response to intervention RtI/problem-solving process: Essentials.* Author, Greenwood Village, CO, 2006.

Tool 4.2

Family-School Partnering (FSP)

Teaming Interventions: What Families Need to Know

TEAMING INTERVENTIONS FOR STUDENT SCHOOL SUCCESS

WHAT FAMILIES NEED TO KNOW ...

1. You are a very important and equal member on your student's team.
2. You are a critical part of the decision making about your student.
3. You and other team members will look at current achievement, set goals, prescribe interventions, and monitor progress.
4. Call yourself a partner and use words such as "we," "us," and "our."
5. Share your knowledge. You know your student best. Discuss strengths, challenges, attitude about school, school history, and homework habits.
6. Try to attend all meetings. If you cannot, ask about ways to participate through calls, out-of-school meetings, e-mails, or home visits.
7. Ask if there is a specific school staff member with whom you can communicate about your student and the teaming process.
8. Observe your student and ask him or her about current learning experiences.
9. Tell your student that you are teaming with the school to help him or her succeed.
10. Always ask questions if you do not understand.
11. Ask how your student will be included in the teaming process.
12. Much teaming occurs outside meetings at both home and school; ask how you can help at home in a way that can work for your family.
13. You will be given copies of your student's plan and progress data.

Family-School Partnering (FSP) is sharing responsibility for a student's school success.

Source: Adapted from Colorado Department of Education, *Family and community partnering: "On the team and at the table,"* Author, Denver, CO, 2009.

Tool 4.3

Family-School Partnering (FSP)

Teaming Questions for Families and Educators to Ask Together

ARE WE FOLLOWING THE STEPS?

✓ Define?
✓ Plan?
✓ Implement?
✓ Evaluate?

ARE WE CLARIFYING ROLES AND RESPONSIBILITIES?

✓ Are the family, teacher, student, and any appropriate community resources "on the team and at the table"?
✓ Does everyone have information on his or her roles and responsibilities?
✓ Are we including the student appropriately?
✓ Is there support for the teacher, interventionist, family, and community resource in being team members, if needed?
✓ Are home and school learning being coordinated?

ARE WE SHARING DATA?

✓ Do we have all the data we need to prescribe an intervention, including that from the teacher, family, and student? If not, what are we missing?
✓ Are we implementing jointly understood diagnostic/prescriptive assessment if needed?
✓ Are we using mutually collected data to make decisions?
✓ Are all partners receiving copies of plans and data?

Source: Adapted from Colorado Department of Education, *Family and community partnering: "On the team and at the table,"* Author, Denver, CO, 2009.

Tool 4.4

Family-School Partnering (FSP)

Team Family Information

Student Name: _____ Date: _____
School: _____ Grade: _____
Family Member(s) Completing Form: _____

When is the best time for you to partner with school staff? _____Before School _____ After School _____ Early Evening _____ Preferred Days of the Week

How is it best to communicate with you (for e-mail please specify preferred address; telephone; written notes; in person)?

What are your child's strengths and interests? (These can be at school or home, in any area.)

Do you have any academic or behavior concerns about your child? If so, please identify.

Please share any other information about your child that might be helpful in understanding his or her school life.

Please tell us about the following areas:
Homework:
Previous school history (including any special programs):
Attitude about school:
Special support outside school (tutoring, therapy, etc.):
What has helped in your student's learning? What has not been helpful?
Past or present medical issues:
Other:
What information, support, or materials would be helpful to you and your student?
What else would you like to know?

Please share any other information that you think will be helpful in supporting your child's school success. Feel free to attach additional information or use the back of this sheet.

Source: Adapted from Cherry Creek Schools, *Response-to-intervention RtI/problem-solving process: Essentials,* Author, Greenwood Village, CO, 2006.

Tool 4.5

Family School Partnering (FSP)

Team Intervention Plan With Strengths and Family Coordination

Page _____

Name of Student _____ ID Number _____ DOB _____

Strengths:	Date Identified:
Specific Areas of Focus:	

<table>
<tr><td rowspan="8">Intervention</td><td colspan="7">Research-Based Prescriptive Intervention:
(Specific Curriculum/Program and /or
Instructional Strategy)</td></tr>
<tr><td>Date From:
To:</td><td>Grade(s)</td><td>School/Setting</td><td>Title of Provider</td><td>Hrs/W</td><td>S/T</td></tr>
<tr><td colspan="6">Specific Measurable Outcome:</td></tr>
<tr><td colspan="6">**Family–School Coordination and Communication**</td></tr>
</table>

			Date	Score
Progress Monitoring	Measurement Tool:			
	Frequency of Measurement:			
	Targeted Outcome Data Point:			
	Baseline Data:			
	Interim Data:			

Evaluation	Was the intervention carried out as planned?		☐ Y	☐ N
	Why or why not?			
	Has the student benefited from the intervention?		☐ Y	☐ N
	Has the specific measurable outcome been attained?		☐ Y	☐ N

Recommended Action:
☐ Continue Current Intervention   ☐ Alternative Intervention (Details)
☐ Outcome Achieved   ☐ Diagnostic-Prescriptive Assessment (Details)
☐ Other (Describe under Details)
Details:

Intervention Facilitator:

Source: Adapted from Cherry Creek Schools, *Response to intervention RtI/problem-solving process: Essentials,* Author, Greenwood Village, CO, 2006.

Tool 4.6

Family-School Partnering (FSP)

Permission for Diagnostic/Prescriptive Assessment

Student's Name: Grade: DOB:
School: Date:

(Please note: This permission for diagnostic/prescriptive assessment is to be reviewed and discussed with a family as a component of ongoing communication and student success planning.)

Dear _____,

Our school is committed to supporting student school success. If a student struggles in academics or behavior, it is important for school personnel and families to work together. You are invited to partner in the planning and monitoring of your child's targeted interventions as a team member. The quality and effectiveness of interventions for your child will be strengthened by your input and participation. To better prescribe interventions, specific assessment is sometimes recommended to learn more about a student. We would like to collect the following information about your student at this time:

Specific area of concern:
Purpose of assessment:
Specific assessment tools/staff involved:

I give permission for my child to participate in the above-named diagnostic/prescriptive assessment. I understand that I will be given an explanation and copies of assessment results. Also, I know that I will be able to partner with school staff on recommendations from the assessment to help coordinate learning between home and school.

Please share the following with us:
I need more information on the following:

It would be helpful for you to know this about my student:

Parent/Guardian Signature _____ Date _____
Family Intervention Liaison _____
Telephone: _____ E-mail: _____

Source: Adapted from Cherry Creek Schools, *Response-to-intervention RtI/problem-solving process: Essentials,* Author, Greenwood Village, CO, 2006.

Tool 4.7

Family-School Partnering (FSP)

School-Home-School Note or Home-School-Home Note

Definition: A school-home-school note serves as a teamed, two-way communication and intervention system. It can identify, monitor, and support a student's new learning behavior at school or at home. Both academic and behavior skills can be addressed.

STEPS TO ESTABLISHING A SCHOOL-HOME-SCHOOL NOTE

- Have a conversation between teachers and family members.
- Include the student in explaining and planning as early in the process as is appropriate.
- Identify strengths and prioritize concerns.
- Select skill areas to be developed.
- Determine how home-school goals will be defined and measured.
- Determine the criteria for success.
- Design the school-home-school note with two-way communication capacity, including the student in the plan.
- Establish responsibilities.
- Identify possible rewards for home and school with student.
- Establish a reward system.
- Monitor and modify the system according to data.
- Provide feedback for everyone.
- Troubleshoot, maintain, or fade as needed.

Name: _____   Date: _____

Name: _____   Date: _____

Home and School GOAL (S)	School Period #1	School Period #2	School Period #3	Homework	Other
	0 1 2	0 1 2	0 1 2	0 1 2	0 1 2
	0 1 2	0 1 2	0 1 2	0 1 2	0 1 2
	0 1 2	0 1 2	0 1 2	0 1 2	0 1 2
TOTALS					

Teacher Initials _____   _____   _____
Family Initials   _____   _____
Student Initials _____   _____   _____   _____
Successess and Comments: _____
_____

Goal for Today: _____%
Total for Today: _____%

```
        KEY
0 = No
1 = Somewhat....
2 = YES!!
```

Source: Adapted from Colorado Department of Education. *Family and community partnering: "On the team and at the table,"* Author, Denver, CO, 2009.

Five

Planning FSP Actions

Data are necessary to calibrate perception... The collection, examination, and interpretation of data inform continual improvement efforts.

Wellman & Lipton, 2004

Chapter 5 summarizes various family-school planning ideas in the literature, relating these to recommended practices for sustainable system change. The importance of job descriptions and the family-school partnering (FSP) collaborative consultant role is discussed. A simple, cyclical, data-driven action-planning process is presented.

After reviewing this chapter, the reader will

- Name essential elements for sustaining FSP implementation
- Describe FSP job descriptions, including that of FSP collaborative consultants
- Understand the data-driven FSP action-planning rationale and cycle

Action planning for FSP stems from sustainability principles recommended in the system reform literature. The problem-solving process seen in many response-to-intervention (RtI) frameworks provides familiar cyclical steps to integrate various sources of tiered data, strategically planning FSP and student school success. Simplicity and diverse applicability are goals of our FSP action planning.

FAMILY-SCHOOL PLANNING MODELS

Several family-school initiatives that have been described in the literature incorporate important components of planning and implementation. Each has unique contributions regarding how a school community might begin to focus on FSP. All can serve as a resource for schools considering the shift to tiered partnering, depending on the area of focus.

Constantino (2003) identified the family friendly school's five-step model for implementing engagement initiatives: awareness, self-assessment, program conceptualization and development, program implementation, evaluating, and sustaining. Recommendations for implementation were phrased in terms of questions for stakeholders, and the importance of concrete visible actions was highlighted. Minke (2008) stressed careful planning because of the pervasive sensitivity needed to build trusting family-school relationships. In *Partnerships by Design*, Ellis and Hughes (2002) highlighted linking partner planning to existing documents and priorities, such as school improvement plans, school newsletters, curriculum guidelines, and demographic information. According to Ellis and Hughes, "Planning is all about taking your vision and turning it into reality" (p. 4). They included several key planning elements, including defining current status and goals and anticipating barriers. Outlining the details of partner roles and evaluating success are crucial in their process. The final steps are advertising results and revising according to data. In *School, Family, and Community Partnerships: Your Handbook for Action,* Epstein and colleagues (2002) provided an explicit planning process for working with families and schools, including such details as meeting formats, goal forms, and funding requirements focused on her six types of parent involvement. Training and surveying stakeholders were stressed. A compilation of planning tools, attitude measures, and partnering ideas to fit various school communities is seen in *Beyond the Bake Sale: The Essential Guide to Family-School Partnerships* (Henderson et al., 2007). There is a strong focus on building a shared understanding of academic, social-emotional, and behavioral expectations and the role each partner plays in their attainment. The authors recommended assessing current attitudes and practices to determine how ready a school is for FSP. Once this information is obtained from all families and school members, a team is assigned to help prioritize needs, strengths, and strategies. A multipurpose family-school team was also recommended by Christenson and Sheridan (2001). Their suggested teams use a standard problem-solving model to identify priorities, analyze resources and constraints, brainstorm alternatives, select specific strategies, develop an action plan, and implement a chosen procedure.

SYSTEM REFORM

FSP can be conceptualized as systemic educational reform.
For many educators and families, shifting from a more traditional parent involvement model to one that focuses on
shared responsibility between home and school is a significant change in practice. Implementing new initiatives is
challenging, and certain actions support successful shifts.
Frameworks for system change vary, but work by Curtis,
Castillo, and Cohen (2008) emphasized a typical problem-
solving model that involves "switching the direction" to goal
setting for desired outcomes by asking questions: What is the
current status? Why is it this way? What should be done about
it? Did it work? Focusing on data use, measurable outcomes,
evidence-based processes or actions, and formative evaluation
are all key features of system change. Ervin and Schaughency
(2008) summarized important change factors as the following: motivation to change; perceived effectiveness and acceptability of the new practice; and knowledge, skill, and sense of
efficacy regarding practice implementation. They pointed out
that the closer a new behavior or skill is to perceived current
and effective practices, the easier it is to accept. Integrating
FSP into current structures and practices helps acceptability
and familiarity.

   In applying these findings to FSP implementation, it is recommended that all stakeholders receive common information about the legal, research, and reform rationale so that
the need to shift behavior is understood. Knoff (2008), in
discussing systemwide behavioral support systems, pointed
to the importance of having "blueprints" to guide efforts and
informed facilitators, who continually reinforce and educate
stakeholders. Ongoing colleague support can provide the necessary new learning opportunities for educators (Knoff, 2008;
Schmoker, 2006). Schmoker (2006) also stressed the importance of a results focus, regular follow-up, and adjustment
according to data. Lasting change requires the integration of
new practices into the existing culture and operational norms
(Raines, 2008). Three of Fixsen, Naoom, Blasé, Friedman, and
Wallace's (2005) implementation cornerstones are directly
applicable to the FSP shift: (a) coordinated training, coaching,
and formative assessment; (b) organizational infrastructure
that can provide timely instruction, support, and outcome
evaluation; and (c) full involvement of interested and invested
constituent groups.

Roles and Responsibilities

Clearly identified FSP role expectations, when embedded into job descriptions, can often lead to more comprehensive, schoolwide practices (Christenson, 2004). FSP roles and functions will be more readily embraced (a) when viewed as a natural part of existing job expectations versus if they are seen as "additional," unsupported job responsibilities and (b) when sufficient information and support are provided so that individuals feel competent in their ability to engage in these new responsibilities (Ervin & Schaughency, 2008). In addition, new FSP roles are more readily adopted when rationalized with empirical evidence that highlights the positive impact of FSP on relevant educational outcomes (Christenson, Godber, & Anderson, 2003).

The success of FSP efforts depends on many individuals, including school administrators, teachers, staff support professionals, as well as family organizations, individual family members, and students. Administrators play a distinctive role by ensuring that FSP is embedded into the mission, policies, and annual goals of the school; by prioritizing and communicating high FSP expectations; and by demonstrating the importance of FSP in everyday practice. Frontline staff members ensure that families feel welcomed, respected, and cared for and promptly receive clarification and requested information. Teachers and other educational professionals often play key roles in explaining and sharing expectations about FSP in homework and daily learning. They also engage in ongoing two-way communication with students and families. School mental health professionals, because of their training in understanding data, facilitating meetings, and designing interventions, often take on consultative, supportive, and educative roles to promote FSP in all tiers. School-based family organizations, such as parent-teacher associations (PTAs), have moved beyond a sole focus on fund-raising to embrace leadership roles on key family-school committees, reinforcing the focus on student school success, and reaching out to all families. Finally, family members play an important role through direct and indirect participation in their child's school, by requesting and sharing information with teachers, and by creating home environments that support and coordinate learning.

A brief, open-ended survey was given to over 200 school administrators, teachers, and mental health professionals who attended a series of state-sponsored workshops on family involvement (C. Lines, personal communication, May 26, 2009). Attendees were asked to identify the unique contributions each partner makes to enhance family-school partnerships. The results of this survey correspond to other work documenting distinct FSP roles and functions (Christenson, 2004). These role descriptions are briefly described next. In Tables 5.1 and 5.2, these results are summarized for school staff and for families, students and community resources, respectfully, with specific job descriptions listed to further elaborate these roles and functions.

FSP Leadership

In addition to the suggested job descriptions, it is important to note the importance of strong leadership in implementing and successfully sustaining FSP. Curtis et al. (2008) identified the need for a "gatekeeper" who has decision-making power, the ability to allocate resources, and authority within the system. Because the FSP focus is on schools, families, and students, tapping leaders from each of these groups is ideal. School principals and leadership teams must be familiar with the legal, evidence, and reform base of FSP. They will need to learn, understand, and support action planning, resource reallocation, and everyday practice shifts. Focusing on the strong relationship of FSP to academic achievement is often a motivating factor for school leadership. Diverse family representation will provide guidance and support families in partnering with teachers around their student's success. Again, knowledge of the FSP rationale and specific information about their role is key for families. Tapping student organizations and student leaders to advocate for partnering, reach out to staff and family members, and support each other in school success can be powerful in enacting lasting changes in a school and in the future educational worlds.

FSP Collaborative Consultation

Because FSP may be new for staff, families, and community resources (Chavkin, 2003; Manz et al., 2009), assigning facilitators, or what we like to call "FSP collaborative consultants," is a helpful action supported in the professional development (Schmoker, 2006; Stollar et al., 2008) and system change work (Curtis et al., 2008; Fixsen et al., 2005; Knoff, 2008). This role would be specifically defined by needs and resources but would most likely require skill in facilitation,

Table 5.1   Family-School Partnering (FSP): Partnering Job Descriptions for School Staff

Building Administrators

✓ Communicate FSP rationale and philosophy to staff and families.

✓ Prioritize FSP for staff and expect shifts in practices, responsibilities, and time.

✓ Ensure teachers and family access FSP training and ongoing support.

✓ Supervise FSP and include as a staff performance appraisal standard.

✓ Include partnering "on the agenda" in all meetings and in all policies and publications.

✓ Ensure family participation in school decision making.

✓ Focus on positive FSP efforts and recognize those participating.

Classroom Teachers

✓ Engage in two-way communication and relationship building with all families.

✓ Utilize team interventions with families when a student is struggling.

✓ Highlight FSP for students.

✓ Share class rules and homework expectations with students and families.

✓ Encourage learning discussions and support at home, with linkages to school.

✓ Provide positive feedback to families about student school success.

Educational Specialists (Advanced Learner Educators, Special Educators, Interventionists)

Same as for classroom teachers.

✓ Explain specific role and expertise to families and community team members.

✓ Apply specific skills to teaming interventions.

✓ Coordinate team interventions between home and school.

School Mental Health Professionals (School Psychologists, Social Workers, Counselors)

✓ Serve as FSP collaborative consultants to staff and families.

✓ Support schoolwide universal, targeted, and intensive FSP practices and processes, focusing on school success.

✓ Connect families with community resources and provide education.

✓ Provide conflict resolution services.

✓ Team with language and cultural liaisons in family outreach.

✓ Apply specific skills to teaming interventions.

✓ Encourage communication about strengths.

"Frontline" Staff (Clerical, Custodial, and Cafeteria)

✓ "Meet and greet" all families when in building.

✓ Welcome family volunteers.

✓ Provide expertise in ensuring all families have access to needed services.

✓ Ensure all family questions are answered.

Source: Adapted from Colorado Department of Education, *Family and community partnering: "On the team and at the table,"* Author, Denver, CO, 2009.

Table 5.2 Family-School Partnering (FSP): Partnering Job Descriptions for Families, Students, and Community Resources

Families

✓ Participate in ongoing two-way communication and relationships with teachers, sharing successes and concerns.

✓ Support learning at home by communicating about school with frequent and systematic discussions, encouraging schoolwork, providing resources, and supervising (personally or with resources) homework, TV viewing, and afterschool activities.

✓ Ask school for help and support when needed.

✓ Utilize team interventions with teachers when a student is struggling.

✓ Highlight FSP for students.

✓ Know and support class rules and homework expectations.

✓ Give positive feedback to school staff when possible.

Students

✓ Know that the school values home-school partnering.

✓ Share with home about school and school about home, including completing home and class learning assignments.

✓ Know and advocate for own learning needs at home and school.

✓ Participate in teaming own interventions if appropriate.

Parent-Teacher Organization

✓ Reach out to all families and include in school community building.

✓ Support tiered partnering practices that focus on student school success.

✓ Provide family expertise and "family-to-family" support.

✓ Provide family education opportunities.

✓ Create a "family center" in the school.

✓ Recognize positive FSP efforts.

Community Resources

✓ Know the rationale and philosophy of FSP.

✓ Support schools and families in communicating and collaborating concerning student school success.

✓ Team in planning and implementing student interventions.

✓ Recognize positive FSP efforts.

Source: Adapted from Colorado Department of Education, *Family and community partnering: "On the team and at the table,"* Author, Denver, CO, 2009.

consultation, data use, and systemwide interventions. Such consultants would also need to have FSP knowledge, tools, and resources. Administrative support and legitimacy of the assigned responsibilities would be necessary. Kampwirth (2006) defined *collaborative consultation* as "a process, in which a trained school-based consultant working in an egalitarian, nonhierarchical relationship with a consultee, assists that person in efforts to make decisions and carry out plans that will be in the best educational interests of students" (p. 3). Thus, a person in this position would focus on student school success by facilitating partner education, supporting adults learning new practices, helping groups and individuals action plan, and being available to all parties as needed. FSP would be on this consultant's "responsibility plate." The expectation would be that he or she would champion the cause throughout the system, individually and within groups, by helping problem solve issues, sharing success stories, offering training, and addressing hurdles. In addition, this role could serve to centralize data for others to access and use in their efforts—providing a "vortex" of information. This FSP consultant would collaborate with both school staff and families.

A school mental health professional would be a likely candidate for this FSP collaborative consultant role. School counselors, social workers, and psychologists usually do not have daily classroom responsibilities. Also, interpersonal and facilitation skills are often a component of their training. All three disciplines have ethical codes and practice standards that endorse the collaborative work with families and staff around student success (American Association of School Counselors, 2004; National Association of School Psychologists, 2000 National Association of Social Workers, 2002). These professionals show strong interest in collaborating with families and teachers but are often limited in their time to do so because of other responsibilities, lack of training or self-efficacy, and perceived lack of permission from administration (Christenson, Hurley, Sheridan, & Fenstermacher, 1997; Manz et al., 2009; Pelco, Jacobson, Ries, & Melka, 2000). Strong encouragement to support FSP is offered for school psychologists (Christenson, 2004), counselors (Van Velsor & Orozco, 2007), and social workers (Harris, Franklin, & Hopson, 2007). We recommend that school mental health professionals put FSP "front and center" on their agendas. They can assess their current practices and needs for training, work with school leadership to reallocate responsibilities to this endeavor, and integrate FSP into their everyday operations. School mental health professionals can model FSP by always inviting a family and student voice to the table in meetings and intervention planning.

Data-Driven Decision Making in the Tiers

Use of multiple data sources can provide valid input from various stakeholders and allow information access from different venues, from an individual teacher's classroom to a parent-teacher organization. Wellman and Lipton (2004) suggested that each of several dimensions of data adds unique information. Their descriptions provide a menu of options for FSP action planning: *quantitative* data are numerical; *qualitative* data are descriptive; *existing* data are demographic, performance, or documents; *collected* data are gathered and include *monitoring* or *formative evaluation* and are usually either perceptual, such as in surveys, or behavioral, such as in frequency counts or percentages.

In FSP, both adult and student data need to be considered. Adult beliefs and practices need to be identified and incorporated into planning. Specifically, the student school success indicators are defined by identified data sources, such as school attendance and extracurricular involvement. It is always best practice, although not always possible, to triangulate data, which is to use at least three different data sources, usually different types, as no one piece of data can provide a comprehensive picture of an issue (Raines, 2008; Wellman & Lipton, 2004). In a similar vein, disaggregating or breaking down data allows for looking at patterns and differential effects for subgroups. Another caveat about using data effectively is to provide visual displays whenever possible. Not only do visual displays have the power to improve performance (Miller & Kraft, 2008), but also when examined together by partners or groups they allow for objective, shared decision making in which all parties have equal access to the same information (Wellman & Lipton, 2004). Visual data are more easily understood and used effectively. All of these points about helpful data use apply to both the FSP action-planning process and work with individual students.

Finally, the universal and targeted-intensive FSP tiers can have unique data sources and action-planning cycles. This allows allocation of resources and time according to the specific outcomes sought with more intentional measurement of effective actions. Tier processes and practices can be utilized in prioritizing goals and identifying potential data sources for each tier. It is crucial that all tiers be considered in planning an integrated, strategic plan. The *FSP Tiered Guide* provides a data road map tied to specific processes and practices in each tier. This guide allows for ongoing planning, with revisions based on data.

Check Out This FSP Tool: *FSP Tiered Guide*

FAMILY-SCHOOL PARTNERING ACTION PLANNING

A critical dynamic underlying an effective FSP framework is a strategic implementation process. Data, ongoing support, and linking to current initiatives are used to plan and monitor identified aspects of FSP. As described, there are several comprehensive systemwide family involvement formats in the literature, but implementing partnering initiatives has remained difficult and elusive for many school communities (Christenson, 2004). In striving for easy and effective FSP implementation, the action-planning process in this book attempts to link resources, time, and data to existing information and infrastructures. The process does not recommend or require development of a new team or organizational body. Instead, FSP action planning should be addressed within existing groups and by individual partners. By continually evaluating efforts, revision can occur so that time is not wasted on ineffective practices. Also, by having established a common rationale and philosophy for the shift to FSP, it is hoped that schools can move in a focused direction to assess their current status and desired outcomes. Each stakeholder must understand his or her FSP job responsibilities as well as how they are part of a larger effort. Ongoing support to both school staff and family members helps to ensure transition fidelity and system sustainability.

Action-Planning Cycle

A familiar and simple four-step cycle can be used to guide implementation of the FSP framework. This four-step process can be applied to partnering efforts by individuals, teams, committees, organizations, or entire schools. There is a strong emphasis on flexibly utilizing diverse data types, which are either existing or collected.

Our suggested FSP action-planning cycle is pictured in Figure 5.1. The first two steps of the cycle are preparatory stages, *define* and *plan*, using data from multiple sources. The third step, *implement*, acts on the specific goals, assignments,

Family-School Partnering (FSP) Action-Planning Cycle

Share Understanding of FSP Rationale and Philosophy

DEFINE
1. Collect and Review Data
2. Map Strengths and Resources
3. Identify Hurdles

PLAN
1. Prioritize Measurable Goals
2. Identify Actions and Interventions
3. Assign Responsibilities, Resources, and Timelines
4. Choose Measurement Tools

EVALUATE
1. Assess Goal Attainment and Implementation
2. Revise Plan
3. Continue

IMPLEMENT
1. Follow Plan as Intended
2. Monitor Progress

Figure 5.1 Family-School Partnering (FSP) Action-Planning Cycle.

and actions and then objectively measures progress. Finally, the last step, *evaluate*, involves assessing effectiveness by reviewing and sharing data, discussing fidelity of plan implementation, and continuing with a revised plan. This cyclical process is an automatic, data-driven methodology useful to many aspects of school life, not just FSP. The four steps are cyclical and continuous, so that ongoing adjustment of time and resources can occur as guided by data. Each step is further elaborated next and incorporated into an action-planning form.

Check Out This FSP Tool: *FSP Action Plan*

Share Understanding of FSP Rationale and Philosophy

The arrow to the left side in the action-planning visual of Figure 5.1 describes the base for the implementation cycle. For FSP, the legal mandates and strong research supporting increased student school success as a result of FSP should be shared with all parties. Effective and sustainable shifts in practice require "buy-in" and a reason to operate differently (Johns et al., 2008; Raines, 2008). The legal, evidence, and reform rationale for FSP is strong and convincing, but it must be shared in a timely, respectful manner with school staff and families so that action planning and implementation will be genuine, meaningful, and understood.

DEFINE: Collect and Review Data; Map Strengths and Resources; Identify Hurdles

Diverse types of data from numerous sources, which can be triangulated and analyzed, provide planning guidance. In FSP, both adult and student data are utilized. Student school success data sources are disaggregated regarding ethnicity, home language, socioeconomic status, grade, and disability. Family participation percentages, disaggregated in the same way as student data, provide both a baseline and an ongoing measure of partnering during such activities as conferences, events, volunteering, school visits, returning surveys, and intervention teaming. At this stage, collecting opinions and then openly conversing about possible FSP hurdles are strongly recommended so that solutions to address these can be included in planning. A status check of current practices, areas of expertise, FSP interest, existing materials, and funding sources is obtained and shared with stakeholders to identify existing FSP practices and experiences. A key to successful implementation is tapping and allocating current resources wisely. FSP data tools, in this book and the accompanying CD, provide choices for schools, depending on identified needs, resources, and goals. They may be used at any of the four action-planning steps, but it is often during the initial defining of FSP that tools are reviewed and accessed selectively. Suggested tools for each step are highlighted in boxes in this chapter.

Check Out These FSP Tools (Existing Data): *FSP Document Checklist, FSP Existing Teams and Meetings Chart, FSP Strength and Resource Map, FSP School Data Snapshot*

Check Out These FSP Tools (Collected Data): *FSP Partnering Survey and Needs Assessment, FSP Student Viewpoint, FSP Hurdles and Solutions, FSP Disaggregated Participation Percentages, FSP Event Feedback, and FSP Teaming Feedback*

PLAN: Prioritize Measurable Goals; Identify Actions and Interventions; Assign Responsibilities, Resources, and Timelines; Choose Measurement Tools

The use of SMART goal setting is recommended for FSP action planning as it acts as a simple acronym that focuses on measurability and accuracy. SMART is a common term that has several variations, but the one we are recommending here is specific, measurable, attainable, relevant, and time-based. Strategies, actions, and interventions should be chosen because of their importance, acceptability, and availability (Cherry Creek Schools, 2006). They should have evidence of relevance and success. They should be worded in specific, objective terminology. It is important that responsibilities, resources, and timelines are all realistic. Measurement of all plans should be objective, simple, and tied to both baseline and expected outcome levels.

IMPLEMENT: Follow Plan as Intended; Monitor Progress

Specific actions, responsibilities, resources, and timeline guide implementation. It is important that those responsible for plan actions receive appropriate training, support, and recognition. Using appropriate data collection tools as defined in the plan will allow for credible decision making at the next step or sometimes during the implementation phase. Following the plan as it was developed should be the intent, with any changes noted.

EVALUATE: Assess Goal Attainment and Implementation; Revise Plan; Continue

Success is evaluated. Ineffective actions need to be examined and revised according to data. Implementation fidelity needs to be assessed. A plan should be discontinued if formative data or stakeholder feedback provide evidence of ineffectiveness or harm. Results of an action plan need to be used in continued planning for the future. Visual data will help decision makers understand information and use it to make decisions. Joint examination of data, with discussion, will lead to more successful next steps and further FSP improvements.

Using the FSP Action Plan

The FSP action-planning process occurs at each tier and with individuals. The process can be used with currently functioning teams, organizations, and meetings. Examples of school and family working groups who can use the action cycle are administrative teams, grade-level teams, academic departments, parent-teacher organizations, safety and crisis teams, problem-solving teams, special education staffing teams, professional learning communities, community outreach groups, as well as individual teachers, administrators, and support staff. The action plan can be used in performance appraisals, in professional growth plans, and to review current efforts. For example, instructional teams or departments may decide how they want to implement homework completion plans consistently. Parent-teacher organizations can discuss partnering roles as far as supporting family-to-family outreach or family centers. Communication about such planning can occur during faculty meetings and be announced in newsletters, on Web sites, or in e-mails. Table 5.3 shows an example of FSP action planning, data use, and evaluation for a high school special education team wanting to increase family-school coordination of student interventions.

KEY TERMS

- **Action plan:** An action-planning document that can be used by a school, committee, team, or individual.
- **Action-planning cycle:** A four-step, widely applicable process—*define, plan, implement,* and *evaluate*— that can be applied in any situation to activate FSP or other initiatives; also is a key component of teaming student interventions at the targeted-intensive tiers.
- **FSP collaborative consultation:** Having a designated, knowledgeable person to support FSP throughout the everyday practices of a school; school mental health professionals are recommended for this role based on their professional preparation and commonly assigned responsibilities.
- **SMART goals:** A common goal-setting acronym to guide the action-planning process; specific, measurable, attainable, relevant, and time-based are the descriptors chosen for FSP outcome expectations.
- **Visual data display:** Graphs, pie charts, pictographs that provide focus, joint information to guide partners in shared discussions and decision making; allows for objective discussion, focuses on results, and reduces conflict.

Table 5.3 Family-School Partnering (FSP): High School Special Education Action Plan Example

School: *High School* **Group/Team/Committee/Individual:** *Sped Team* **Date:** *12/09* **Page:** *1*

DEFINE. Identify and attach applicable data sources: *Percentage of families included in assessment, goal, and school-home planning: 4%; mean family and team satisfaction rating on FSP Teaming Feedback 1.8*

PLAN. Prioritize measurable goal(s): 1. *100% of families with students in special education process will participate in assessment and IEP goal planning.* **2.** *Team member satisfaction mean rating will be 4.0 (6.0 being highest rating) for all participants.*

IMPLEMENT- Actions and Interventions:	Responsibilities ("Who Will Do It?")	Resources (Funding, Time, People, Materials)	Timeline (Day, Month, Year)	Measurement Tools/Data: (Pre- and Post-action, Intervention; Monitoring)
1. Obtain every family's input regarding assessment needs, goals, and school-home coordination prior to any special education actions or meetings.	Case managers or teachers	30 minutes per week of individual time; compensated if necessary by early depart option	6/10/10	Pre 12/2/09: 4%; Post 5/30/10: 76%
2. Ask each multidisciplinary team member to complete FSP Teaming Feedback after meetings.	School mental health professional	Clerk support: 10 minutes a week for data collection and recording	6/10/10	Mean team member satisfaction: Pre 12/5/09: 1.8; Post on 5/30/09: 4.1

(Continued)

Table 5.3 Family-School Partnering (FSP): High School Special Education Action Plan Example (Continued)

EVALUATE. Assess goal attainment (Were the goals reached according to the data?) **and implementation** (Were the actions implemented as planned?):

1. Goal not attained, but significant growth over a five-month period; 72% increase in special education family participation.

2. Goal attained; average satisfaction rating was increased by 2.3 on feedback survey. YES, action plans were implemented as planned.

Revise plan and continue:

During 2010–2011 school year, with a 6/10/11 timeline: Goals 1 and 2 will be continued; Goal 3 will be developed based on review of existing special education student homework completion data.

1. Continue with same data collection procedures. Family participation will be 100%.

2. Continue with same data collection procedures. Team member satisfaction mean will be 5.0 (6.0 being the highest rating) for all participants.

3. Students in special education programs will complete 75% of their homework assignments each week (pre-action data 32% homework completion average). School-home-school note system will be implemented with 100% of families and case managers.

Source: Adapted from Jennings, D., *RtI implementation planning tool.* 2008. Retrieved April 8, 2009, from http://www.tacommunities.org/document/list/p/folder_5071%252Ffolder_5073%252Ffolder_5162.

TOOL DESCRIPTIONS

Action Planning

FSP Tiered Guide. This guide is intended to help school communities plan and sequence their FSP work.

FSP Action Plan. This plan is intended to be simple, implementable by individuals or groups, and tied to key FSP components; this action plan serves as a planning template.

Existing Data

FSP Document Checklist. This adaptable list is intended to guide school and family teams in integrating FSP terminology and actions into all school communications and procedures.

FSP Existing Teams and Meetings Chart. Each school team, committee, and organization is asked to assess current level of FSP and plan accordingly so that FSP can be naturally integrated.

FSP Strength and Resource Map. By asking about staff and family members in the school community, this tool identifies potential leaders, trainers, and collaborative consultants.

FSP School Data Snapshot. These data points are used to guide school communities in organizing existing and collected data to plan FSP and assessing student school success.

Collected Data

FSP Partnering Survey and Needs Assessment. This survey assesses staff and family member FSP beliefs and practices in a parallel format; a needs assessment with preferred times and venues is included.

FSP Student Viewpoint. Asking students about their FSP perceptions and ideas is the focus of these adaptable questions.

FSP Hurdles and Solutions. This open-ended document asks stakeholders to identify hurdles and solutions at individual and school levels.

FSP Disaggregated Participation Percentages. In planning and evaluating FSP, it is important to analyze data from various perspectives, and this document serves as a guide.

FSP Event Feedback. This is a brief, multipurpose survey, tapping stakeholder (including staff, students, and family member) feedback about events.

FSP Teaming Feedback. This brief survey is intended to obtain participant feedback when teaming interventions, including various types of planning, such as in RtI, special education, or individual learning plan.

RESOURCES
Web Sites

American School Counselor Association: http://www.schoolcounselor.org/index.asp

Provides information for professionals and families on the role of the school counselor. Includes a section responding specifically to parents.

National Association of School Psychologists: http://www.nasponline.org

Provides information for professionals and families on the role of the school psychologist. Includes a position statement on partnering with families and numerous resources on diverse, related topics.

School Social Work Association of America: http://www.sswaa.org

Provides information for professionals and families on the role of the school social worker.

Books

Schmoker, M. (2006). *Results now: How we can achieve unprecedented improvements in teaching and learning.* Alexandria, VA: Association for Supervision and Curriculum Development.

Focuses on how schools can improve teaching and learning. Includes such topics as literacy, professional learning communities, and leadership.

Wellman, B., & Lipton, L. (2004). *Data-driven dialogue: A facilitator's guide to collaborative inquiry.* Sherman, CT: MiraVia.

Surveys the various uses of data in supporting school improvement. Describes various data sources, searching for patterns, teaching about data. Includes practical tools.

[handwritten: Define = self assessment tool]
[handwritten: qualitative data — families, school, staff about processes being used.]
[handwritten: data collection tool]

Tools 5.1–5.12

Tool 5.1

Family-School Partnering (FSP)

Tiered Guide

Directions: Please check if in place and list appropriate information to guide FSP planning. Add information as needed and update according to data. Each tier includes previous tiers.

Date: _____   Person(s)/Team Completing Form: _____

FOUNDATION

Philosophy
—Student school success is the center of family-school partnering
—Education is a shared responsibility between home and school
—Families and educators each bring unique expertise and cultures

List Practices (such as sharing in school publications and staff/ family trainings):

List Data Sources:

UNIVERSAL TIER

Processes
—Build Relationships
   —Take Time
   —Show Respect
   —Recognize Efforts
—Create Welcoming Settings
   —Address Environment
   —Recognize Alternative Opportunities
—Use Two-Way Communication
   —Offer Options
   —Focus on Positives
   —Invite Responses
—Educate Partners
   —Cultivate Shared Understanding
   —Increase Confidence

List Practices (such as interactive homework, two-way post-cards, family sharing sheets):

List Data Sources:

TARGETED-INTENSIVE (UPPER) TIERS
Process **—Team Interventions** 　—Implement Teaming Four Steps – DEFINE, PLAN, IMPLEMENT, EVALUATE 　—Clarify Roles and Responsibilities 　—Use Shared Data **List Practices (such as RtI problem-solving teams with families, school-home-school notes, conjoint behavioral consultation):** **List Data Sources:**

Source: Adapted from Colorado Department of Education, *Family and community partnering: "On the team and at the table,"* Author, Denver, CO, 2009.

[handwritten annotation: experiential — use @ mtg. the mtg.]

Tool 5.2

Family-School Partnering (FSP)

Action Plan

School: _____ Group/Team/Committee/Individual: _____
Date: _____ Page: _____

DEFINE. Identify and Attach Applicable Data Sources:

PLAN. Prioritize Measurable Goal(s):

IMPLEMENT. Actions and Interventions:	Responsibilities ("Who Will Do It?"):	Resources (Funding, Time, People, Materials):	Timeline (Day, Month, Year):	Measurement Tools/Data (Pre- and Post-Action, Intervention; Monitoring):
1.				
2.				
3.				
4.				

EVALUATE. Assess Goal Attainment (Were the goals reached according to the data?) **and Implementation** (Were the actions implemented as planned?):
1.
2.
3.
4.
Revise Plan and Continue.

Source: Adapted from Jennings, D. (2008). *RtI implementation planning tool.* Retrieved April 8, 2009, from http://www.tacommunities.org/document/list/p/folder_5071%252Ffolder_5073%252Ffolder_5162

Tool 5.3

Family-School Partnering (FSP)

Document Checklist

Directions: Please check if component or action is included in document or communication and if representative family members have reviewed. Please note date reviewed or revised.

in education of family school partnerships

Schoolwide Documents	Includes FSP Philosophy: Student Success Focus; Sharing Responsibility and Cultures	Includes Two-Way Communication Capability	Reviewed by Family Members for Clarity and Helpfulness
Handbooks: student, staff, family			
Discipline and attendance procedures			
Web site			
Newsletter			
Student intervention team			
Procedures			
Other:			
Classroom Documents			
Class and homework procedures			
Classroom management description			
Letters home			
E-mail system			
Problem-solving strategies			
Grading procedures			
Homework examples			
Other:			

Tool 5.4

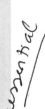

Family-School Partnering (FSP)

Existing Teams and Meetings Chart

Directions: Please check whether each team or meeting currently includes family-school partnering (FSP) in planning, actions, and agendas. Then, if yes, please describe those activities; if no, identify how FSP might be included in the group's work.

Date: _____

Team/Person(s) Completing Form:_____

Team or Meeting	Does This Team Include FSP in Planning and Actions? Please Check If Yes.	If Yes, Identify Actions and Planning. If No, Describe Ways to Include FSP.	If Yes, Identify Involved Staff and Families. If No, Identify Who Will Be Participating.	If Yes, List Data Used in FSP Decision Making. If No, Please Describe Possible Data Tools and Use.
Leadership team				
Grade-level/ academic teams or departments (specify):				
School improvement committee				
Student intervention teams (specify):				
Professional learning communities (specify:)				
Parent-teacher organization				
Other (continue with all existing meetings/teams)				

Tool 5.5

Family-School Partnering (FSP)

Strength and Resource Map

Directions: Please identify school staff, families, or community members who have expertise or an area of interest in the following areas to help in FSP implementation.

Date: _____

Team/Person(s) Completing Form:_____

FSP Expertise or Area of Interest	Which School Staff, Family Member, or Community Resource?	Which Specific Topic Area, Program, or Practice?	Availability
Literacy partnering			
Math partnering			
Social-emotional-behavioral partnering			
Family-school partnering (FSP) facilitation			
English language learners and diverse culture partnering (specify languages/cultures)			
Other			

tool for identifying members on vaction planning team

[handwritten margin notes: "define + evaluate" "quantitative data—" "demographic data to collect."]

Tool 5.6

Family-School Partnering (FSP)

School Data Snapshot

Directions: Use these data as a baseline and monitoring tool to guide your FSP planning.

School: _____ Date: _____ Data Time Period: _____

DEMOGRAPHIC PERCENTAGES

1. Ethnicity
2. English Language Learners
3. Free and reduced lunch
4. Special program student participation (include special education and identify other programs)

DISAGGREGATED STUDENT SCHOOL SUCCESS FACTOR PERCENTAGES

Grade, Disability, Ethnicity, ELL, Free and Reduced Lunch, Department/Classroom

High School Completion
- Graduation rate

Continuous Academic Progress
- Academic achievement assessments
- Benchmarks and progress monitoring
- Grade averages
- Credit completion

Engaged Learning
- Homework completion
- Classwork completion
- Attendance
- School event participation

Prosocial/Coping Skills
- Suspensions
- Expulsions
- Office referrals
- Suicide assessments
- Threat assessments
- Extracurricular involvement
- Observation rubrics
- Teacher and student ratings

Tool 5.7

Family-School Partnering (FSP)

Partnering Survey and Needs Assessment

Directions: Our school is developing new ways to partner with families to best support our students' school success. This survey was developed to gather data about our current family-school partnering (FSP) practices from all stakeholders who support our students. Please answer questions from your perspective or role. There are four sections to the survey. Section 1 is for everyone, **Family Members and School Staff.** Section 2 is for **Family Members only.** Section 3 is for **School Staff only.** Section 4 is for everyone, **Family Members and School Staff.** We welcome any and all comments or ideas. We will use this information to help guide our future FSP efforts. Thank you for your support!

_____ School Staff   Position: _____
_____ Family Member Role: _____
_____ Student   Grade Level: _____
Date:_____

I would like to participate on a family-school partnering committee at our school.

My contact information is as follows (name, e-mail, phone, or address):
Name (Optional): _____
_____

Please share any comments or ideas you have in the space below or throughout the survey regarding how our school can best support families and teachers in working together to coordinate student school success.

Source: Adapted from Colorado Department of Education, Family and community partnering: "On the team and at the table," Author, Denver, Co, 2009.

Thanks to the family members, professionals, and graduate students who provided input as to this survey's content.

SECTION 1: FAMILY MEMBERS AND SCHOOL STAFF

BELIEFS (WHAT I THINK ...)

I ...	N/A	Strongly Disagree	Disagree	Undecided	Agree	Strongly Agree
1. Believe that families and schools share responsibility for a student's education.	0	1	2	3	4	5
2. Believe that students should see their teachers and families working together in relation to their everyday school experiences and learning.	0	1	2	3	4	5
3. Believe that schools and families each have areas of expertise/information to share in supporting student success.	0	1	2	3	4	5
4. Believe teachers and family members should communicate regularly about both positive events and concerns.	0	1	2	3	4	5
5. Believe that teachers and family members should share concerns when either sees a student beginning to struggle or get discouraged.	0	1	2	3	4	5
6. Believe that teachers and family members should plan interventions together when concerns are identified.	0	1	2	3	4	5
7. Believe that students should be partners in home-school communication and in intervention planning.	0	1	2	3	4	5
8. Am confident in my ability to develop and maintain family-school partnerships in my specific role (as school staff or family member).	0	1	2	3	4	5
9. Have time to develop family-school partnerships in my specific role (as school staff or family member).	0	1	2	3	4	5
10. Have the skills/training to work as a partner in supporting school success for students.	0	1	2	3	4	5

Comments:

SECTION 2: FAMILY MEMBERS ONLY

Practices (What I Do ...)

I ...	N/A	Not at All	Rarely	Sometimes	Frequently	Very Frequently
1. Encourage my student to do his or her best in school and ask about school activities and learning.	0	1	2	3	4	5
2. Take time to find out about my student's school, classes, activities, school rules, and expectations for homework.	0	1	2	3	4	5
3. Communicate regularly (two way) with teachers for positive reasons, routine matters, and concerns if needed.	0	1	2	3	4	5
4. Share my student's strengths, challenges, interests, and attitudes about school with the teachers.	0	1	2	3	4	5
5. Monitor and provide resources, time, and space for homework or seek community/school support to help.	0	1	2	3	4	5
6. Ask teachers what I can do to support my student's learning at home or through community resources.	0	1	2	3	4	5
7. Problem solve with teachers when there are academic or behavior concerns about my student.	0	1	2	3	4	5
8. Tell my student that the school and our family are working together to help him or her be successful.	0	1	2	3	4	5
9. Welcome visits to my home from school staff.	0	1	2	3	4	5
10. Visit and volunteer at my student's school and classroom.	0	1	2	3	4	5

Comments:

SECTION 3: SCHOOL STAFF MEMBERS ONLY

Practices (What I Do ...)

I ...	N/A	Not at All	Rarely	Moderately	Frequently	Very Frequently
1. Provide information to families on how to support and encourage their student, access resources, and talk about school and learning.	0	1	2	3	4	5
2. Find ways to reach out to families with cultural, language, gender, socioeconomic, and learning differences.	0	1	2	3	4	5
3. Communicate regularly with the families of all my students for positive reasons, updates, and to ask for their feedback.	0	1	2	3	4	5
4. Ask each family to share ideas about their student's strengths, challenges, interests, and attitudes about school.	0	1	2	3	4	5
5. Use data from multiple sources when I discuss a child's progress, needs, problems, and possible solutions.	0	1	2	3	4	5
6. Include families in any discussion or problem solving about their student when I have any academic or behavioral concerns.	0	1	2	3	4	5
7. Ask families what they need to actively support student learning in the home or with community resources.	0	1	2	3	4	5
8. Specifically call or invite families to events at the school.	0	1	2	3	4	5
9. Visit families in their homes.	0	1	2	3	4	5
10. Tell my students that the school and their families are working together to help them be successful in school.	0	1	2	3	4	5

Comments:

SECTION 4: FOR FAMILY MEMBERS AND SCHOOL STAFF

A. I WOULD LIKE MORE INFORMATION ABOUT ...

- Sharing responsibility for student's learning
- Creating learning opportunities at home or with community resources
- Parenting
  - Communicating
  - Supporting learning at home
  - Teenage years
  - Other (please share topic): _____
- Teacher-family communication
- Homework success strategies
- Family volunteer opportunities from home or at school
- How to be involved in school decision making, leadership
- Teachers and families working together when a student is struggling
- Area community resources
- Conflict resolution strategies
- How to meet other families at the school
- How to communicate with staff or families to support FSP
- Other (please identify): _____

B. BEST TIMES AND WAYS TO COMMUNICATE WITH ME ...

- Weekday mornings (before school)
- Weekday afternoons (after school)
- Anytime during the school day
- Weekday evenings
- Saturdays
- Online
- Phone calls
- Direct visits to my home or school
- Written materials
- With notes brought home or to school by students
- Watching a video
- Communicate with other families or teachers
- Other (please identify): _____

C. WHAT WOULD BEST HELP ME TO BECOME A BETTER PARTNER IS ...

- Time to contact each other directly
- Interpreters on site
- More convenient times
- Travel assistance to and from the school
- Child care during meetings
- A place to meet and network with other families or teachers
- Other (please identify): _____

[handwritten notes in top margin:] student govt → student project / student representative on family engagement + planning team

Tool 5.8

Family-School Partnering (FSP)

Student Viewpoint

Directions: Our school is learning more about how families and teachers work together to support our students' school success. We would like to know how students see our school. Please check the activities you have seen in your classroom, home, or school this year.

Grade:_____ Date: _____

____ 1. My family has come to the school. *[handwritten:] → doesn't say much about it.*
____ 2. My family has met my teachers.
____ 3. My teacher and family talk to each other when I do good things at home or school.
____ 4. If I need help or have a problem, my teacher and family talk about it.
____ 5. My family knows our school and classroom rules.
____ 6. My family knows what I am learning at school.
____ 7. If there is a problem with my homework, my family, teachers, and I discuss how to solve it.
____ 8. Someone from school has visited our home. *[handwritten:] ✎ ——*
____ 9. I get special help at school if I need it, and my family knows about this.
____ 10. Someone helps my family members understand about school in the language they understand.

Please write down three ideas about how families and schools can work together to help students.

1.

2.

3.

[handwritten notes in right margin:] — how accurate

— does student have accurate parent understanding of school if not clear/sure?

○ fewer student reflect class/parent involvement.

• may need to simplify response to family/make easy

[handwritten note at bottom:] lacks action plan in response

Tool 5.9

Family-School Partnering (FSP)

Hurdles and Solutions

Directions: A *hurdle* is defined as a "difficulty or obstacle that has to be overcome". (Merriam-Webster, 2004). Please identify what you see as the two greatest hurdles for you and your school in family-school partnering (FSP) at this point in time. Please consider time, logistics, knowledge, past experiences, and role expectations. Then, generate at least one possible solution for each of your identified hurdles.

Person(s) Completing Form: _____

Role: School Staff _____ Family Member _____ Student _____

	Hurdles	Solutions
Individual	1. 2.	1. 2.
School	1. lack of convenient time to meet 2.	1. 2.

Source: Adapted from Colorado Department of Education, *Family and community partnering: "On the team and at the table,"* Author, Denver, CO, 2009.

[handwritten margin notes:] useful as needed — esp if set goals to engage family but not meeting those goals — esp if goals to be participate in family literacy nights

triangulating data from across student groups.

qualitative

Tool 5.10

Family-School Partnering (FSP)

Disaggregated Participation Percentages

Directions: Please note family participation percentages for each group and event.

Date: _____ Person/Team Completing: _____
Time Period: _____

FSP Activity (Specify)	Number Attending	Ethnicity (Identify) (%)	Free and Reduced Lunch (%)	Home Language (Identify) (%)	Classroom (Identify) (%)	Grade (Identify) (%)	Students With Disabilities (Identify) (%)
School event:							
Family-teacher conferences:							
Family-teacher organization:							
At school volunteering opportunities:							
Surveys or information gathering:							
Individual student team meetings:							
School committees:							
School visits:							
Home visits:							
Other:							

Tool 5.11

Family-School Partnering (FSP)

Event Feedback

Directions: Our school is working on developing positive family-school partnering (FSP) to support student success. This feedback survey was developed to gather staff, student, and family feedback about their experiences during family-school events. Please share your thoughts with us. Thank you for your time. Please also share any other ideas about this event.

Name (Optional): _____ **Date:** _____

Role: Staff Member_____ **Family Member** _____

Community Resource _____ **Student** _____

Date of Event: _____

Type of Event (Please Identify): _____

_____

Please circle the number for each of your responses below.

	Very Strongly Disagree	Strongly Disagree	Disagree	Agree	Strongly Agree	Very Strongly Agree
1. I knew about the event in advance.	1	2	3	4	5	6
2. I received a personal invitation to attend the event (via e-mail, call, written note).	1	2	3	4	5	6
3. I understood the purpose of this event.	1	2	3	4	5	6
4. I know how this event supports my student's (or if student, my) learning.	1	2	3	4	5	6
5. I was able to get to know others from the school (i.e., school staff, family members, students) at this event.	1	2	3	4	5	6
6. I felt welcome at this school event.	1	2	3	4	5	6
7. I was able to share my ideas at this event.	1	2	3	4	5	6
8. I was able to get all my questions answered at this event.	1	2	3	4	5	6
9. I was glad I came to this event.	1	2	3	4	5	6
10. I think this event should be continued in the future.	1	2	3	4	5	6

Comments or ideas for the future:

Tool 5.12

Family-School Partnering (FSP)

Teaming Feedback

Directions: This survey was developed to gather staff, family, and community resource feedback about partnering during individual student planning. The planning process may have been by telephone, e-mail, postal service, face-to-face conversation, or meetings involving several people. Thank you for your time in letting us know about your experience. Please share any comments with us.

Name (Optional): _____**Date:** _____
Role: Educator _____ **Family Member** _____
Community Resource _____ **Student**_____

INDIVIDUAL PLANNING PROCESS
(PLEASE CHECK ONE)

___ RtI (Response-to-Intervention Plan)   ___ ALP (Advanced Learning Plan)
___ IEP (Individualized Education Program)   ___ ILP (Individualized Learning Plan)
___ Teacher-Family Plan   ___ Conjoint Behavioral Consultation
___ FBA (Functional Behavioral Assessment)/   ___ Wraparound
    BIP (Behavior Intervention Plan)
___ Other (Please Identify):

Please circle the number for each of your responses below.

	Very Strongly Disagree	Strongly Disagree	Disagree	Agree	Strongly Agree	Very Strongly Agree
1. I shared my information and perspective in the discussion.	1	2	3	4	5	6
2. Written information and progress data were given to me and fully explained.	1	2	3	4	5	6
3. I was considered in decision making.	1	2	3	4	5	6
4. I know what goals we are working on together and how we will decide if the plan is working.	1	2	3	4	5	6
5. I know how I can support my student's learning.	1	2	3	4	5	6
6. There is a two-way communication plan in place.	1	2	3	4	5	6
7. I felt like a full team member when we were discussing my student.	1	2	3	4	5	6

Comments:

Source: Adapted from Colorado Department of Education, *Family and community partnering; "On the team and at the table,"* Author, Denver, CO, 2009.

Six

Applying FSP Lessons

Hurdlers know there will be several obstacles ... they plan ahead as to how to overcome. With a little foresight ... there can be successful navigation.

Adapted from Ellis & Hughes, 2002

Chapter 6 describes commonly cited individual and school hurdles to implementing family-school partnering (FSP). We explore potential solutions in overcoming hurdles in three ways: true stories explaining how FSP can work in schools; evidence-based programs, which have clear instructions and proven effectiveness; and frequently asked questions (FAQs). After reviewing the chapter, readers will

- Name the commonly encountered hurdles to FSP implementation
- Plan for hurdle navigation by knowing true stories, evidence-based programs, and FAQ answers
- Generate possible solutions to hurdles

To fully engage in FSP, specific hurdles must be overcome. Assessing personal beliefs, taking risks, and opening up oneself to diverse opinions are all components of the honest exploration of FSP barriers. It is important to learn from others who are practicing FSP, explore explicit programs that have undergone experimental rigor, and answer the most frequently asked questions. Students will benefit from their families and schools partnering together, even when there are struggles. A commitment to this student-focused FSP vision will be the first step appearing on the path to successful FSP practices, allowing for successful navigation of the inherent challenges.

DEFINING FSP HURDLES

With such a clear rationale, based in the law and research, why are many educators and families hesitant to engage with each other in genuine, ongoing, meaningful partnerships? Numerous researchers have identified barriers to implementing FSP (Christenson, 2004; Christenson & Sheridan, 2001; Esler et al., 2008; Hoover-Dempsey et al., 2005).

We are choosing to reframe barriers as "hurdles" as this allows for action planning in overcoming such blocks and achieving intended goals. We borrow our rationale from Ellis and Hughes (2002) and include their thinking:

> Sprinters take off from the blocks and run straight ahead, trying to reach the finish line before the other runners. Any obstacle that gets in their way will keep them from reaching their goal in a timely manner, and, at times, may keep them from finishing the race. Hurdlers, on the other hand, know that there will be several obstacles placed between them and their goal. They look at these obstacles as a way to sharpen their techniques and increase their skills. They plan ahead as to how to overcome these obstacles in a way that will enhance their ability to reach their goal. Part of putting together a workable partnership plan is to forewarn of possible "hurdles" along the way and formulate responses to them. (p. 37)

Christenson (2004) described structural barriers and psychological barriers for both educators and families. Structural implies such concrete factors as lack of time, funding, communication systems, transportation, and training. Psychological is used to describe barriers that are attitudinal in nature, such as self-efficacy, role confusion, linguistic and cultural differences, fears of conflict, and ambiguity about FSP. Similarities in barriers experienced by educators and families have been articulated, and in summarizing from our experiences, the most common mutual challenges seem to be the following: lack of time for communication and developing relationships, logistical barriers such as transportation and language differences, lack of partnering training or knowledge, lack of self-efficacy rooted in personal history, and unclear role expectations. Esler et al. (2008) stressed the importance of openly identifying and addressing the most prevalent barriers for school communities, individual teachers, and family members. System and personal open reflection around challenges leads to productive insight, discussion, and potential solutions. Also, experts agree that it is the responsibility of a school to provide leadership in resolving both family and staff partnering concerns (Christenson & Sheridan, 2001).

In addition to the issues mentioned, our work has provided insights into factors that seem to most frequently interfere with FSP implementation. We have chosen to summarize these, including some previously mentioned, for both school staff and families together, categorized as *individual* and *school hurdles* to most easily lead to solutions. Simple, concrete examples of hurdles and solutions are summarized in Table 6.1.

NAVIGATING HURDLES

FSP hurdles may be different for each school staff and family member, depending on unique histories, traditions, cultures, and practices. It is difficult to generalize from one situation to another except to strongly recommend that individuals and schools assess their status and respond accordingly. Then, depending on the identified issues, steps can be taken toward establishing focused solutions. Table 6.2 depicts a school staff member's assessment.

The FSP framework, as described in this book, was designed to directly provide stakeholders with a rationale and practical tools to address typical challenges seen in the field. By using tiers, data, and a student school success focus, the intent is to provide multiple ways to support the shift in thinking from traditional parent involvement to FSP. Also, by strongly stating the importance of integrating FSP into existing practices, permission is given to continue ongoing established operations with the added focus on FSP. A new structure does not need to be created. In addition, stating the legal and research rationale of FSP is integral, as is providing some means of ongoing encouragement from identified family and school staff members, both in everyday conversations and in more formal support structures such as FSP collaborative consultation. Personal solutions can be applied to individual concerns, and systemic ones are undertaken by school, family, or community organizations. School mental health professionals or FSP collaborative consultants can provide support concerning identifying and navigating both individual and school hurdles. Brainstorming, "thinking out of the box," and sharing stories can be helpful in finding solutions (Ellis & Hughes, 2002).

Table 6.1 Family-School Partnering (FSP) Common Hurdles with Sample Solutions for Families and Schools

COMMONLY-CITED HURDLES	SPECIFIC EXAMPLES	POSSIBLE SOLUTIONS
TIME Individual (School Staff or Family Members)	• Workload demands	• Prioritize FSP as important for a student's school success • Reassess commitments • Shift time from another activity • Coordinate with other staff or family members • Pool resources
	• Scheduling conflicts	• Brainstorm alternatives • Find nontraditional time and "space" • Use phone, video, or computer technology
School	• Other mandated priorities	• Prioritize FSP as important for student success • Create flexible staff hours to match family availability • Identify family drop-in hours
	• Set, contracted hours	• Compensate staff for FSP time • Allow for home or community visits • Rotate work schedules for additional coverage
LOGISTICS Individual (School Staff or Family Members)	• Transportation	• Share rides • Coordinate with community resources • Offer bus passes • Compensate cab fares • Explore alternative off-site meeting options such as home visits, community centers, libraries

	Barrier	Strategies
School	Language differences	• Access school or community volunteer interpreters • Bring trusted family member, friend, or colleague • Use translation headphones • Provide or request translated copies of all routine and important documents
School	Limited funds for interpreters	• Collaborate with community resources • Find and train community volunteers • Utilize carefully selected college/high school students for extra credit
	Limited staffing for adding FSP responsibilities	• Shift or reallocate roles and resources • Reprioritize job responsibilities • Seek out community resources and supports • Train family members to assist with FSP activities
KNOWLEDGE Individual (School Staff or Family Members)	Unsure of FSP skills	• Access FSP information from public or internet resources • Initiate learning communities or book clubs on FSP • Inquire about FSP workshops or classes • Ask for support from an identified mentor • Role-play unfamiliar situations
	Lack of confidence	• Ask colleagues, family members, community resources for tips • Meet in comfortable venues • Seek out personal feedback • Offer informal "drop-in" or "getting-to-know-you" times for family and staff sharing and informal conversation
School	Limited staff and family understanding of FSP	• Plan opportunities for conjoint and/or separate staff and family FSP trainings • Offer training in multiple venues and multiple times • Identify FSP as an annual school reform or professional development goal • Develop a collaborative, tiered FSP school and district model

(Continued)

Table 6.1 Family-School Partnering (FSP) Common Hurdles with Sample Solutions for Families and Schools (Continued)

COMMONLY-CITED HURDLES	SPECIFIC EXAMPLES	POSSIBLE SOLUTIONS
EXPECTATIONS Individual (School Staff or Family Members)	• Unaware of accessible FSP information	• Set up an FSP hot-line or resource area • Make relevant web sites available to all • Initiate family-to-family and staff-to-staff FSP collaborative consultation • Ask district or school to identify an FSP coordinator • Regularly review one new FSP resource at existing school-wide and committee meetings
	• Unsuccessful previous school and/or family-school partnering experiences	• Provide testimonials about successful FSP • Infuse FSP into familiar situations, such as "Back-to-School-Night" or PTA/PTO meetings • Seek comfortable, individualized opportunities to begin FSP • Focus on identifying common "dreams and hopes" for a student's future success
	• Traditional role perceptions	• Include FSP in job descriptions, performance appraisals, and family-school communication • Engage in active FSP team decision making • Ask families to review any materials to be sent home for FSP role description • Ask each teacher and family to communicate about FSP roles throughout the year • Link positive student/family and staff outcomes to FSP
School	• Limited staff, family, and community buy-in	• Share the FSP legal and research rationale • Provide data-based evidence of positive, successful FSP • Assess staff and family FSP attitudes and needs • Evaluate and revise FSP efforts based on existing and collected data
	• Lack of existing FSP infrastructure	• Infuse FSP into policies, procedures, and agendas • Adapt existing written manuals, handbooks, and school publications to include FSP • Create ongoing performance expectations and school-wide evaluations that include FSP

Table 6.2 Family-School Partnering (FSP): Individual Example of Hurdles and Solutions

Directions: A *hurdle* is defined as a "difficulty or obstacle that has to be overcome" (Merriam-Webster, 2004). Please identify what you see as the two greatest hurdles for you and your school in family-school partnering (FSP) at this point in time. Please consider time, logistics, knowledge, and expectations. Then, generate at least one possible solution for each of your identified hurdles.

Person(s) Completing Form: TL

Role: School Staff ___X___ Family Member _____ Student _____

	Hurdles	Solutions
Individual	1. Not enough time.	1. Schedule 30 minutes a week (one half of a planning period) for FSP activities (such as calling families, writing notes, planning interactive homework).
	2. Feel anxious about talking to families when students are struggling because I feel like a failure.	2. Talk to a colleague about strategies; contact all families initially so a relationship is established, making it more comfortable to problem solve; start with positives; ask family to partner; focus on student success.
School	1. Many staff members do not see partnering with families as a component of their job descriptions.	1. Share information on the legal and research rationale for FSP; include in performance appraisals; put in job descriptions; provide collaborative colleague consultation to support staff in shifting to FSP.
	2. Many families work long hours away from school.	2. Offer multiple times for school events, including weekends with flexible staff hours; do "outreach conferences" at homes and at work sites; use creative personal communication venues such as texting, e-mail; ask families what works.

STORIES FROM THE FIELD

Implementing FSP is new for many families and educators. Stories from the field can offer concrete, practical road maps for stakeholders as they work together in reaching their identified partnering goals. Also, stories can develop understanding of the positive results seen in a partnering framework. Several brief scenarios are provided to represent different voices. The vignettes address the commonly cited hurdles: time, logistics, knowledge, and expectations. The core facts are taken from actual situations, with some supportive material added to highlight relevant topics from the field. Lessons learned are summarized to provide guidance to practitioners.

High School Teaching With an FSP Twist

HURDLES ADDRESSED: TIME, EXPECTATIONS

An English teacher at a large high school teaches advanced placement classes. During her third year of teaching, she was telling her supervisor, as they were reviewing her performance appraisal, that she really worried about some of her students and was not sure she had "permission" to contact parents directly to share her concerns as the message seemed to be that student independence was primary. Her supervisor pointed out the specific rubric on the teacher appraisal form that stated, "Building positive family-community relationships." He suggested that at the beginning of the next school year she call the families of all her students, leave a message introducing herself, share her openness to communication, and request a contact if ever there were concerns or feedback. Her initial reaction was that there would never be time to implement the plan. However, she thought it over and then decided to try it with at least one class. Then, after realizing she could leave messages quickly with each family, she decided to go ahead and call the families for all the students in her five classes. The calls took approximately 3 hours, over 2 weeks, for 150 families. She reported the results as "amazingly positive" in that she did frequently hear from families with questions or just to share information. Her students, who did not believe her plan as no one had ever tried it before, were responsive and open about how it was a relief to talk honestly with their now-more-informed parents. Students also were humorous about the recent conversations, joking that they now "have something to talk about with their parents at dinner." She reported that there was early home-school communication for any kind of learning or behavioral issue.

The teacher, who had been thinking of leaving education for another profession, had her best year ever, feeling supported by her students and families. She has since committed to a teaching future. Most students demonstrated strong achievement on college assessment measures, with a few struggling students receiving targeted home-school-community support. A key data point was the increase in timely homework completion from previous years.

She and her supervisor shared the story with other faculty as a procedure to optimally enact the appraisal policy and support FSP for students at the high school level. Now, the department is thinking of having a student "partnering advisory board" that would help teachers and families share information productively. Students on the board could help devise forms and technology as well as gather information about college or postsecondary options. An additional strategy that arose from the discussion was to develop an e-mail list for the families in each class (with preferred contact information for families who do not have e-mail access), sending weekly communication describing class activities and learning data. Students are copied on the e-mails so that they can participate in the discussion and information sharing. The teacher summed it up as, "I think the rewards for this activity are felt by us all—me, the students, and their families. We all feel engaged in the learning process and we are working together."

LESSONS LEARNED

- Teachers sometimes need to "jump over" hurdles to gain confidence and experience the time shift needed to engage in FSP; a "push" from a supervisor can help.
- Including FSP expectations in performance appraisals can encourage action.
- High school students and their families respond to communication and teacher outreach, defying the myth of "total independence" from school support.
- Proactive teacher-family contact supports immediate early intervention if a student begins to struggle.
- Teachers and family members find personal and professional gratification from partnering relationships.
- Students enjoy watching adults in their lives work together.

School Mental Health Professionals Just Do It

HURDLES ADDRESSED: TIME, LOGISTICS,
KNOWLEDGE, EXPECTATIONS

A school psychologist had one family class in his graduate training; the class was focused on students with disabilities. He was serving three elementary schools and concerned about the apparent "blaming" and "family bashing" he observed in meetings and informally in the lounge. A counselor also worked at one of his schools, and a local mental health center had placed a licensed clinical social worker at another school. He teamed with these other two school mental health professionals on a regular basis and decided to talk with them about his concerns. The three school mental health professionals resolved to do some research on FSP models and activities. After consulting with colleagues and professional sources, they decided as a team to begin explicitly including families in their everyday work to model and support other staff in seeing the value of working more openly with families. Overwhelmed with daily demands, they realized their efforts had to be manageable and easily implemented to succeed. They all first talked to building administrators, who were supportive but also clear that all typical job responsibilities needed to continue as previously established.

The following partnering strategies were incorporated into their everyday work. They provided classroom and small group curricula "family practice" sheets for all social skills being learned during such sessions as bully prevention and conflict management; families and students were asked to do home review, practice, and then communicate feedback to teachers or school mental health staff. The professionals decided to communicate individually with family members before their student was discussed in a special services care-and-concern meeting; families were invited to participate and share information as part of the team; the school mental health professionals worked with classroom teachers and other educational specialists to support their comfort with this new process. It was decided to publish a series of short articles in the school newsletter and on the Web site about the value of learning support at home, stressing three simple daily supports: talking to your child about school, encouraging effort, and providing after school time and place for homework completion. Families were invited to review existing data and discuss assessment questions with the professionals before a psychological assessment for special education eligibility or reevaluation occurred. Interested teachers were encouraged to contact all families personally through phone calls, e-mails, or postcards and to develop two-way communication structures.

Based on requests from several parent-teacher association (PTA) families in the three schools, the school mental health professionals offered an evening parenting course, using a curriculum with a research base for their specific population, then taking compensatory time during the day with the permission of the principals. They shifted work hours one day a week to be available to families before (6:30–8:00 a.m. when families bring students to before-school care) or after school (4:00–7:00 p.m.); this expanded availability was publicized to families. Another simple idea was asking family representatives to review forms, communication, family practice sheets, and articles for "family-friendly" language and understandability before distributing to the entire educational community. A suggestion box was placed in the hallways near the main offices where family members, students, and staff could put anonymous suggestions for improving FSP. Monthly early morning coffee times were established where families could "drop in" to meet other families and staff while learning more about the school and partnering opportunities.

At the end of the school year, the three school mental health professionals collected feedback data from students, staff, and families. Those who had participated in the various efforts were positive in their evaluation, stating the clarity of communication and the learning about families or schools, respectively, as being important. Specific student data for students in the care-and-concern process whose families participated were monitored with positive outcomes. The administrators appreciated the data and the generally positive tone observed at meetings and from family members. A broader comprehensive plan will be initiated for the next school year, with some interested families and teachers serving on an FSP school improvement team subcommittee. The plan is to have broader "messaging" about FSP and to offer more personalized support for launching FSP practices in conjunction with more explicit goal setting and data collection.

LESSONS LEARNED

- Small, simple, specific actions can have an effect on systems in support of FSP actions.
- Expanding typical structures and activities to include a family component can be effectively implemented without more resources or time.
- Lack of formal training does not need to be a barrier in developing FSP.
- School mental health professionals can provide leadership and support to others in shifting practices to a partnering base, using data and commitment to the vision.

REACHING OUT TO A FAMILY FROM A DIFFERENT CULTURE

HURDLES ADDRESSED: TIME, LOGISTICS, KNOWLEDGE, EXPECTATIONS

A middle school girl had arrived a year earlier from an eastern European country. She spoke English fluently and reported that she had liked school in her native home. Teachers reported that she seemed distant and disengaged in the learning process. She rarely completed homework, was often found wandering the halls, and tended to ignore adult conversation. Teachers attempted to call home and left messages, but no one responded. There were repeated attempts to talk to the student about her school difficulties, but changes were not observed. The response-to-intervention (RtI) problem-solving team convened to share information and prescribe interventions. The school psychologist and one of the classroom teachers visited the student and her father at home to connect with the family and encourage participation in the problem-solving process. The girl's father, a single parent, welcomed the school contact and agreed to attend the first meeting. The problem-solving team members learned the following information: The student was an only child who studied piano at the concert level, often practicing 3 or 4 hours a day; her mother was killed as they escaped their native country; her father was working a carpentry job in the United States but had been trained as a physician; the student had previously done well in school;

the father had not been to a school site since he was a student; the father was unaware of his daughter's current problems but knew she was not liking school.

The problem-solving team, including the student and her father, met and reviewed information, set measurable goals, decided how to monitor progress, and agreed to meet again. The school had been considering a special education referral, but with the new information decided to partner with the family concerning a specific home-school-home intervention plan, including some diagnostic, prescriptive assessment of her reading skills and emotional status. The father began to cry and thanked the school staff for "so many people caring about my daughter and me—no one had ever done that before." The student cried and said it was so important that "my father came to school and could understand what it was like for me here." The father visited his daughter's classes during the next week and regularly communicated back and forth with school staff, sharing data related to the intervention plan.

LESSONS LEARNED

- Personally reaching out to families and encouraging participation can be effective, efficient, and important in supporting student success; this can be especially true for families with different cultural backgrounds.
- Families often respond to personal invitations and welcome the opportunity to share information about their cultures and their lives.
- Students may not know how to link their families and schools in partnering; they benefit from school staff support in sharing about school.

Teaching FSP to Preservice and Practicing Professionals

HURDLES ADDRESSED: TIME, KNOWLEDGE, EXPECTATIONS

The following opportunities were developed and offered to participants in various venues. Session appraisals were always requested and evaluated, with feedback being integrated to improve offerings. Numerical ratings for the presentations were consistently favorable (C. Lines, personal communication, September 25, 2009).

ESSENTIALS SEMINAR

A four-hour essentials training for preservice, practicing professionals and families was designed to provide key knowledge, rationale, and practices for initiating tiered FSP. The class includes a packet of slides and tiered materials for schoolwide, classroom, team, and organization use. The intent is to make the presentation flexible in format so it can be easily integrated into an existing course or presented in brief portions during faculty or parent-teacher organization meetings over a series of weeks. Learning outcomes for participants are specified. The material can also be adapted for joint use with families or a family-specific course (C. Lines & P. Zimmerman, personal communication, April 25, 2008).

HIGHER EDUCATION COURSE

Developing an in-depth quarter or semester learning experience for undergraduate or graduate students allowed for skill development as well as theoretical and research fluency. Materials allow for differing professional preparation needs (teacher, school mental health professionals, administrator). The syllabus includes family interviewing, consultation practice, and case studies. The tiered, data-driven FSP framework is stressed, with discussion of tools and practices. Identifying and overcoming "real-world" challenges prepares practitioners for the status of partnering in communities that embrace only traditional parent involvement models (C. Lines & G. Miller, personal communication, February 16, 2008).

TRAINING OF TRAINERS

The Colorado Department of Education (2008b) has developed an RtI model for statewide implementation. The model includes six major components, including one of family and community partnership. To provide educator and family training throughout the state, a training of trainers (TOT) module was developed and presented regionally to teams of educators, community resources, and family representatives. The module, *Family and Community Partnering: "On the Team and at the Table"* (Colorado Department of Education, 2009), includes various components that participants can then use to train their own educational communities. Activities, training slides, Web links, and ready-to-use materials for tiered FSP are included. All information is accessible online for electronic availability. Special attention is paid to the shift of teacher-family partnering throughout tiers so that if a child begins to struggle, there is already a co-supportive, mutual, working process in place. Families actively participate in the team problem-solving process for RtI, and if special education is considered, the family is already working with teachers in prescribing and monitoring interventions.

FSP LESSONS LEARNED

- FSP training can be developed and offered in multiple versions and venues to support a shift in practice; flexibility should be incorporated into materials and sessions.
- Trainings can be joint, for families and educators, or specifically geared for a certain group depending on the situation.
- Ongoing evaluation and revision according to feedback is needed for continued effectiveness.
- It is important to honor practitioners' time and provide strategic information based on assessed need as participants vary widely in FSP knowledge and experience.

EVIDENCE-BASED PROGRAMS

In this section, we briefly review three published family-school programs that boast a solid research base and involve families in meaningful ways. These three programs are representative of others cited by various national research review groups. This selected sample is intended to help school practitioners learn about three well-documented FSP models, determine how they embody FSP, and use this established work in their everyday practices. Awareness of specific evidence-based programs can save a practitioner time, lend credibility to FSP implementation, and provide relevant resources to address specific, data-identified FSP needs. These all are potential solutions to commonly cited hurdles in FSP. Resources on where to find additional evidence-based programs are included at the end of this chapter.

The Incredible Years, Check & Connect, and the Achieving, Behaving, Caring Program (ABC) are all described briefly, offering a glimpse into the goals, target audience, process of involving families, and effectiveness data for each program. The programs were selected for several reasons: (a) Each program is considered evidence based as defined by the U.S. Department of Education in terms of strength, relevance, and consistency (Raines, 2008); (b) each program engages families in essential ways with schools; (c) student school success is a focus of each model; (d) FSP processes (building relationships, creating welcoming settings using, two-way communicaton, educating partners, and teaming interventions) are incorporated; (e) explicit instruction and materials are available for implementation; and (f) the programs together target a broad age range and various partnering tiers and are unique from one another in both their goals and application.

The Incredible Years

The Incredible Years has an extensive research base demonstrating skill gains for parents, teachers, and students, specifically in management for adults and improved adaptive behavior for children (Webster-Stratton & Reid, 2003; Webster-Stratton, Reid, & Hammond, 2001). The Incredible Years relies on tenets from social learning theory, with families, teachers, and children all learning skills by watching and modeling real-life examples (Bandura, 1977). The program offers parent, child, and teacher strands and has been selected as a model evidence-based program by numerous groups based on its rigorous study (Webster-Stratton & Reid, 2003). The Incredible Years is targeted at parents who have children ages 0 to 12 years; aims to build such parental competencies as monitoring, discipline, and self-confidence; and increases parent involvement in schooling to decrease problem behaviors. The Incredible Years addresses a variety of skills, including families' understanding of children's developmental levels, modeling social skills, establishing rules and routines, coaching children academically, and developing partnerships with teachers. The program also addresses depressive self-talk as a way of building parents' self-efficacy. Students learn and practice basic social skills. Families and students together learn about the benefits of rules and routines for supporting school success. In addition, families have a better sense of the accuracy of their expectations for their children based on new knowledge of developmental levels.

From an FSP perspective, *The Incredible Years* offers a unique slant on FSP by offering a three-prong approach, involving the student, the student's family, and educators. Families are presented with opportunities to learn parenting behaviors that support student school success. Teachers learn about student motivation, effective ways to collaborate with families, and aligning home and school practices. The third component, the child training program, is designed to strengthen a student's problem-solving and social skill competencies. By addressing all three areas, partners are educated about complementary practices that have been successful. Students, families, and teachers are explicitly taught how to align the home and the school environments. The *Incredible Years* is both skill-based and relationship-based, ultimately teaching both adults and students skills that will allow them to build and strengthen their relationships with others. School staff could potentially serve as trainers for the family and student components in addition to receiving their own training concerning home-school collaboration and student motivation. As staff members work to implement The *Incredible Years* for their families and students, acknowledging and working from the core FSP processes (build trust, create welcoming settings, use two-way communication, educate partners) can go a long way toward heightening the effectiveness of the program.

Check & Connect

Check & Connect has been found to prevent school dropout and to promote school completion (Anderson, Christenson, Sinclair, & Lehr, 2004; Christenson, Thurlow, et al., 2008; Sinclair, Christenson, & Thurlow, 2005). *Check & Connect* draws from theory related to school engagement and resilience and spans academic, behavioral, psychological, and cognitive engagement (Anderson, Christenson, & Lehr, 2004).

The model draws from the basic principles of relationship building and monitoring to help students create enduring positive connections with school. *Check & Connect* is based on the rationale that school engagement and positive connections to school will result in high school completion. The program focuses on promoting positive school-oriented behaviors through a comprehensive mentoring system. *Check & Connect* is targeted for students in kindergarten through 12th grades and is successful with at-risk students and students with emotional and behavioral disabilities based on the time invested from the mentor. One person is designated as the student's mentor and is responsible for modeling engagement, monitoring the student's attendance and academic progress, and developing a trusting relationship with both the student and the student's family. The interventions are designed to be both highly individualized and timely. Skills addressed include relationship building with families, mentors' routine monitoring of potential dropout indicators, regular problem solving with students, and facilitating access to school activities. The model specifically identifies a mentor's daily responsibilities and offers the many ways a mentor can connect with a student and the student's family to promote school engagement.

Check & Connect offers an example of a program aimed at developing close collaboration between the home and school. Mentors assist families and students with different ways to proactively connect to schools when their past experiences with education may have been negative or fraught with stress. The bedrock of *Check & Connect* involves building trust and creating welcoming settings so families begin to see possibilities for partnering. There is explicit teaming for student success, with a focus on such factors as engaged learning behavior and prosocial skills. Mentors are encouraged to work with families for a minimum of two years and to follow students as they transition between programs and schools. Mentors might visit the family's home, make frequent phone calls to discuss the student's progress and needs, or chat informally over coffee. Most important, mentors affirm the unique role families play in their children's education and support families in building their confidence. *Check & Connect* embodies the core FSP philosophy and processes on a daily basis and ensures that families who may have felt disempowered by schools have the opportunity to become partners in their children's education.

Achieving, Behaving, Caring Program

The Achieving, Behaving, Caring Program (ABC) is effective in increasing adaptive social behaviors in students and developing family empowerment in working with schools (McConaughy, Kay, & Fitzgerald, 1999; McConaughy, Kay, Welkowitz, Hewitt, & Fitzgerald, 2008). The program grows from action research theory, a progressive problem-solving approach involving a deepening inquiry into one's own practices or in its participatory forms, the practices of others (McNiff & Whitehead, 2005).

ABC is targeted at schools and families who have young students in elementary school and is based on that idea that social skills, or social competence, in the early years can promote both academic and social development. Overall goals of the program relate to the prevention of emotional or behavioral problems through supporting both academic progress and the development of positive social skills. Building partnerships with parents who are "easy to miss" is also an important tenet of the program. In some *ABC* programs, schools hire a culture broker, typically a parent from the community, to serve as the connection between families and school staff. In addition, parent-teacher action research (PTAR) teams regularly come together to collaborate for children and align the home and school settings. PTAR teams use collaborative action research to first reflect on their own practices of working and interacting with a specific student and then consider ways to shift their practices to better meet the needs of the student. *ABC* also offers the selection of a tailored social skills program as a classroom-specific universal intervention. There are two primary modes of implementation: the school-centered model and the family-school-community model.

ABC offers a unique way to connect families and schools and affect student academic and social-emotional success. Through the action research philosophy, both families and school staff learn to look carefully at the outcomes of their own practices and relationships with children, create mutual goals, engage in ongoing problem solving, and work together to align the home and school settings. All of the FSP processes would be at work in the successful implementation of the *ABC* program. Because school staff and families are asked to both reflect and improve on their own practices, building relationships and creating welcoming settings are especially important for true change to occur. As partners learn about and shift their practices to better meet the needs of a particular child, sharing information can assist others in modifying their own practices. *ABC* is unique in that it encompasses a typical problem-solving model, as seen throughout intervention teaming in FSP, while asking the adults to engage in ongoing self-reflection as a key means for supporting student school success.

FREQUENTLY ASKED QUESTIONS

Frequently asked questions (FAQs) and their answers can help staff and families anticipate hurdles and learn from others. We have summarized the questions we hear most frequently, with answers from experienced partners who adhere to the FSP framework. In answering FAQs, it is important to remember the key FSP tenets: a philosophy of shared responsibility for student school success, tiered opportunities, and data-driven decisions. A brief questionnaire can help individuals, teams, or entire family-school communities proactively answer questions. FAQs are also effective brief exercises in existing meetings, trainings, or other efforts.

 Check Out This FSP Tool: *FSP FAQs: What Are Your Questions and Answers?*

Educator FAQs

1. **How will there be time to partner with families in addition to what already must be accomplished every day?**
   There are no easy answers to this most relevant and important question. A first step is to prioritize FSP in one's own professional life so that time can be shifted and allocated. Suggestions are as follows: Share partnering expectations with all students and families at the beginning of the school year by giving everyone his or her job description; think about all possible communication venues, such as e-mail, postcards, texting, speakerphones, and so on; be proactive by making personal connections with all families at the first of the year, ensuring students and families know homework, attendance, and classwork expectations; think "out of meetings"—important conversations can be held efficiently between two or three people when there is trust and intent to partner; clarify that meetings will be focused and timely, with questions or follow-up happening before or after; think about flexible hours, days, and meeting venues to accommodate families, with compensation time for educators; ask school, family, and community partners how communication and working together can be made efficient, meaningful, and effective; use other resources in the school, such as video recordings of key information taped in various languages; have easy, efficient ways to collect data. Specific FSP tools such as *FSP* ● *Partnering Survey and Needs Assessment* might be helpful in identifying

needs and topics for shared discussions to support shifting time and responsibilities.

2. **When a student is struggling, isn't it more efficient and professional to discuss and plan for student concerns with just specialists first and then contact the family rather than having families participate in initial concern conversations?**

No. The family has important home information to share that provides more accurate data for efficient decision making. By working with school staff in problem solving learning or behavior concerns, families learn how to better support their student at home. Also, school staff can pool resources with the family. In addition, the student sees adults in his or her life working together to support his or her school success. Classroom teachers, who have begun partnering from the beginning, already have relationships with families to mutually address concerns and jointly refer for interventions. *The FSP Family Sharing Sheet* and *FSP Team Family Information* 💿 both offer ways for a family to share how its student learns at home.

3. **How can a school involve families who do not speak English in FSP?**

It is helpful to have a process in place to support families who are English language learners, knowing it is important to help them partner as much as possible. Suggestions include having translated written information (work with others in school or district) and sponsoring available cultural/language liaisons or interpreters (can be family or community volunteers) who establish trust and explain expectations to families. Family-to-family phone trees or home visits can provide volunteer opportunities and meaningful outreach efforts. If there are student academic or social-emotional-behavioral concerns, school mental health professionals working with an interpreter can do an individual interview to support the family in comfortably sharing relevant information. Community resources such as churches and centers can be tapped to support families' comfort in partnering with the school. Including students in the discussions is often a neglected, but effective, strategy. They are bridging both worlds and can share their cultures mutually. Having available tools such as the *FSP Sociocultural* ✎ *Educational Partnering Interview* can offer guidance in culture sharing with families.

4. **How can FSP work in secondary school?**
   Secondary schools have special challenges in implementing FSP. They often have large numbers of students. Teachers are typically trained in subject instruction and have little information about families. Students are becoming more independent in leading their lives but want their families involved in their education (just not at school). Students and families alike respond to school outreach. Providing postsecondary information, considering transition issues, supporting school attendance, and problem-solving homework issues are all important FSP topics for families of older students. Interactive or "teach-to-learn" homework assignments include families in student learning. If a student is struggling, partnering with families immediately is crucial; if there is too much elapsed time, credits toward graduation can be lost, and students can become disengaged. Also, families are the only ones who know a student's history, contributing important information in planning interventions. Another key to successful FSP at the secondary level is to involve students in reviewing communication tools, creating information sheets and invitations, planning class open houses, and serving on "FSP advisory boards." By including students, it becomes "normal" to then directly partner with the family about concerns. Most adolescents enjoy working positively with adults concerning specific goals and activities.

5. **What about family members who demand a certain curriculum, a specific grade, or special treatment?**
   Sometimes, teachers feel bullied or threatened by family members. A universal welcoming and openness to family-school differences is often proactive in preventing these situations. In genuine relationships, partners can share honestly if actions feel uncomfortable. Several strategies have seemed helpful, including using the FSP foundational philosophy that there is shared responsibility for student success, and each

partner has unique expertise. Partners work together in the best interest of the student, and objective data focused on success can be shared as a component of conflict resolution or disagreement. One-to-one meetings over time can be helpful, sometimes away from school. Sometimes, upper-tier conflict resolution protocols need to be implemented, with trained specialists or administrators helping parties successfully communicate and compromise on issues.

6. **What about families who do not return calls, come to school, or answer notes?**
   In a tiered FSP framework, it is expected that 1–15% of families may need individualized encouragement to feel comfortable in FSP. Personal or system hurdles may exist, and these must be understood and navigated. If there is a commitment to working together with families for student school success, there must be allocation of staff and time to consistently reach out to these families in various ways, such as visiting a family in the home. Classroom teachers can receive support from specialists, who team with them in reaching out to hesitant families. "Never give up" is a helpful belief that consistently works to deliver a message of caring to the student and family. Students can sometimes be helpful ambassadors in linking home and school. Deputizing other family members or community resources in helping to develop trust and relationships can also be an effective strategy. It is important to share the school FSP philosophy of partnering with every family for every student's success in conjunction with the legal and research rationale.

Family Member FAQs

1. **If my child is struggling in school, how and when will I know whether or not he or she is making progress if I am part of his or her intervention team?**
   Families are considered equal team members. They help develop interventions, monitor progress, and coordinate learning at home. Families are given copies of plans, data, and other information. It is important to have someone at the school who can answer family members' questions. Ask your school if there is information on how you can support learning at home. *FSP*

Teaming Interventions: What Families Need to Know is a document that explains teaming, and FSP *Teaming Questions for Families and Educators to Ask Together* discusses specific team actions.

2. **Why do I need to be involved if my child is in trouble at school?**
   Students benefit from seeing home and school work together in helping them succeed in school, especially when there are struggles. Families provide important information about what has worked effectively in the past. If a student needs to develop prosocial or coping skills, practicing both at home and at school can be effective. By being a team member in developing interventions, families can coordinate student learning time between home and school. When families and schools work together concerning a struggling student, there are more adults to help, and concerns can be addressed more quickly and effectively. The student sees all adults in his or her life caring about his or her success.

3. **I know my child is struggling in learning, but the school does not seem to think so. What should I do?**
   Family members share in supporting student success and bring unique knowledge about their student. It is helpful to share explicit information with the school about what you observe at home. Also, talking with your child and observing his or her learning can be helpful in collecting data to share with the school. Sometimes, there are differences of opinions, but by working together in setting goals based on data and monitoring progress, shared understandings can occur. Families always have the right to request consideration of special education eligibility. FSP stresses the importance of student school success based on objective criteria so that families and schools can together look at the same data points.

4. **What if I cannot help my child with his or her homework?**
   This is a common event. The most important variables in supporting school at home are talking about school, encouraging learning, and providing structure

for homework completion. Being able to help with the actual content is not necessary as there are teachers at school and community resources to help in that domain. It is important to have two-way communication with teachers about any homework concerns if a student is unable or unwilling to complete homework as this is a component of engaged learning. Teaming interventions with the school, including your student, will be important. It may be that adaptations, specific strategies, or more explicit instructions are needed. There are also some different homework assignments that are specifically focused on families and students working together. These involve your student teaching you new information and are called by such terms as "teach to learn" and "interactive homework."

5. **I do not feel comfortable talking in meetings about my child or in visiting schools as I become very nervous and tend to cry. What can I do because I know it is important for me to be working with the school?**
In partnering, trusting relationships are key, as is two-way communication. This means that sharing your specific concerns and possible solutions with someone at the school is very appropriate. It will be helpful for school staff to know what might create a comfortable situation for you. Suggestions might be to hold meetings in your home or with only one other person, to use a speakerphone, or to ensure that you have all the information in advance. Also, asking to share your thoughts in writing ahead of time can lessen the tension of a meeting. Addressing your student's strengths first in a meeting sometimes instills confidence in family members and is a reasonable request of school staff.

KEY TERMS

- **Hurdles:** Individual and school obstacles to be navigated in developing effective and mutual FSP; key identified hurdles are time, logistics, knowledge, and expectations.
- **Evidence-based programs:** Researched programs that have reliable, trustworthy, and valid evidence to

suggest that they will be effective with specific populations and issues.
- **Frequently asked questions (FAQs):** Questions often posted by educators and families about how to implement FSP.

TOOL DESCRIPTION

FSP FAQs: What Are Your Questions and Answers?
This form can help stakeholders formulate their own
and others' most likely questions about FSP; tenta-
tive answers can then be suggested to aid in planning
and implementation.

RESOURCES
Web Sites

*Center for Effective Collaboration and
Practice:* http://cecp.air.org/center.asp

Facilitates the production, exchange, and use of knowledge
about effective practices in fostering adjustment of children
at risk of developing serious emotional disturbance. Includes
information on the role of schools and families.

Center for the Study and Prevention of Violence (CSPV):
http://www.colorado.edu/cspv/blueprints/index.html

Evaluates prevention programs and identifies those that,
based on "strict scientific standards," are effective in reduc-
ing violent crime, aggression, delinquency, and substance
abuse; includes numerous programs with family and school
components.

Check & Connect: http://ici.umn.edu/checkandconnect/

Describes the research and implementation of *Check &
Connect*, giving the theoretical base and explicit directions
for using the program.

*Collaborative for Academic, Social, and Emotional
Learning (CASEL):* http://www.casel.org

Serves as a resource for evidence-based programs, materials,
databases, policy work, and current information on social and
emotional learning in schools. Includes specific activities and
information related to family participation.

Colorado Department of Education: http://www.
cde.state.co.us/rti/FamilyCommunityToolkit.htm

Provides training information and materials for FSP as related
to RtI; includes TOT slides and presentation notes.

The Incredible Years: http://www.incredibleyears.com/
An extensive Web site with research, training, and implementation information on *The Incredible Years.*

National Registry of Evidence-Based Programs and Practices (NREPP) of the Substance Abuse and Mental Health Services Administration (SAMHSA): http://nrepp.samhsa.gov/
Designed to serve as a comprehensive and interactive source of information for evidence-based substance abuse programs with ratings of individual outcomes. Includes program-specific information on family and school components.

New Mexico Toolkit: http://www.cesdp.
nmhu.edu/toolkit/index.html
Provides an extensive compilation of FSP tools and materials for teachers, families, and professional development. Also available in Spanish.

Promising Practices Network on Children, Families, and Communities: http://www.promisingpractices.net
Highlights programs and practices that credible research indicates are effective in improving outcomes for children, youth, and families. Includes a listing of "proven-and-promising" programs, access to research, and suggestions for effectively implementing programs.

What Works Clearinghouse: http://ies.ed.gov/ncee/wwc/
Established to provide educators, policy makers, researchers, and the public with a central and trusted source of scientific evidence of what works in education. Several topic areas include programs with family participation.

Books
McConaughy, S. H., Kay, P., Welkowitz, J. A., Hewitt, K., & Fitzgerald, M. D. (2008). *Collaborating with parents for early school success: The achieving-behaving-caring program.* New York: Guilford Press.
Describes the *Achieving, Behaving, Caring (ABC)* program in practical, step-by-step terms to guide educators and families in implementation. Includes information on home-school collaboration and training parent liaisons.

Patrikakou, E. N., Weissberg, R. P., Redding, S., & Walberg, H. J. (2005). *School-family partnerships for school success.* New York: Teachers College Press.

Presents FSP research summaries, reports, perspectives, and recommendations from a variety of practical perspectives. Addresses such topics as educator training and grassroots operations.

Raines, J. C. (2008). *Evidence-based practice in school mental health.* New York: Oxford University Press.

Describes how to include evidence-based practices in everyday mental health work, including appraising the literature and evaluating intervention outcomes.

Tool 6.1:

Family-School Partnering (FSP)

FSP FAQs: What Are Your Questions and Answers?

List at least three of your personal or most anticipated questions about family-school partnering (FSP). Please consider possible questions from families, school staff, and students. Then, provide an answer to each question. Developing possible responses can guide your action planning.

1. Q:

    A:

2. Q:

    A:

3. Q:

    A:

Other:

Source: Adapted from Colorado Department of Education, *Family and community partnering: "On the team and at the table,"* Author, Denver, CO, 2009.

Epilogue: A Working FSP School

The vision in writing this book was to craft a simple, clear road map for school communities to follow in implementing family-school partnering (FSP). How did we do? So, what would an FSP school really look like? In answering these questions, we draw from several real situations and create this story of an FSP school, using the practical tools provided in this book. The journey of the school toward FSP is rooted in student success data and fostering shared understanding among families, staff, and students.

ACTION PLANNING

The story includes the following key FSP components: school mental health professionals as FSP collaborative consultants; applying tiered partnering processes and practices; tying FSP to student engaged learning behavior (measured objectively by homework completion) as an indicator of school success; using multiple data sources in planning and evaluating; and integrating FSP into existing family and school structures. The basic FSP action-planning cycle is followed: *define, plan, implement, evaluate.*

Background

This is a typical middle school with sixth, seventh, and eighth grades and 1,000 students. It is located in a suburban metropolitan area. There is a 50% free and reduced-price lunch rate. The ethnic representation is 8% Asian American; 18% African American; 28% Hispanic American; 46% Caucasian. The school is beginning to implement a response-to-intervention (RtI) process for addressing student academic and social-emotional-behavioral concerns. There is a computerized system for accessing grades, attendance, academic achievement, class assignment completion, and discipline data. Seven administrators and assistants compose a leadership team. Of the teachers, 62% have 15 years experience or more. There are five instructional teams for each grade level; these teams meet weekly as professional learning communities. The school has several school mental health professionals: a school social worker (two days a week), a school psychologist (two days a week), and two counselors (full time).

Traditional parent involvement activities are in place, with a parent-teacher organization engaged in fund-raising and volunteer support. There are parent representatives on the school improvement and safety committees. The average parent attendance at school events, conferences, and meetings is approximately 30% of the population, with the exception being back-to-school night, when it is typical to have approximately 60% of parents attending. No difference in participation between grades, ethnic, and socioeconomic groups is apparent from attendance percentage data.

FSP TOOLS USED: *School Data Snapshot, Strength and Resource Map, Disaggregated Participation Percentages*

DEFINE: Collect and Review Data; Map Strengths and Resources; Identify Hurdles

The school mental health professionals (social worker, psychologist, and counselors) are working with the administration and teaching staff on RtI implementation and are collecting information from existing data sources. In their review of student screening data and in tracking referrals to the problem-solving team at the school, they become aware of a significant pattern: 30% of students in each grade are earning at least two failing grades (Fs), which seem directly correlated to homework completion, as seen in student electronic records. They know about the relationship of failing grades to future dropping out of high school and of homework completion to learning engagement. As a result of their data review, the school mental health professionals do a literature search, discuss the issues with colleagues from other schools, and formulate a plan to discuss ideas with their school leadership team. In their initial conversation with administrators, the team is given permission to collect data from families, teachers, and students about how homes and schools currently partner with each other, specifically concerning student school success.

The following data are collected: surveys from staff, families, and students; assessments from current instructional and special team leaders regarding family participation; disaggregated homework completion data. Findings are summarized: family and staff members are similar in reporting positive beliefs about FSP but share few partnering practices; assessed needs are for more information, role clarification, and because time is a significant concern for all stakeholders, that there be some common ground established on this issue; students reported little interaction between families and schools, but suggested such actions as "opening the school more on weekends and telling parents what was expected of us"; professional learning communities and leadership teams do not discuss FSP as part of their work but are open to the idea; the RtI and multidisciplinary special teams do not include family members or students until consent is needed for special education assessment, and then permission is usually sent home with a note of explanation, but there is openness to different practices; 55% of the students in all grades had 95% or better homework completion rates, with no differences in ethnicity, grade, or disability status.

FSP TOOLS USED: *Partnering Survey and Needs Assessment, Hurdles and Solutions, Student Viewpoint, Existing Teams and Meetings Chart, School Data Snapshot*

PLAN: Prioritize Measurable Goals; Identify Actions and Interventions; Assign Responsibilities, Resources, and Timelines; Choose Measurement Tools

The four school mental health professionals include the FSP collaborative consultant role in their job descriptions after discussion with the building principal. Together, this group will serve as a "vortex" for data collection and as supports to staff and families. A simple school action plan is developed based on the compiled data, focusing on families and schools supporting students in homework assignment completion. Data are easily tapped and utilized. The action plan is summarized with the following measurable goal statements:

- FSP rationale will be shared with all staff, families, and students through presentations, Web site, written information, and CD availability by October 1 as measured by attendance, phone or written confirmation, and Web site hit identification. Collaborative consultants, administrators, parent-teacher organization leaders, student council, and technology staff or volunteers are responsible for marketing information and goal completion.

- Each school staff member will complete an individual action plan to include families in partnering for student school success, with a focus on engaged learning, specifically homework completion, by November 1 as documented by plans reviewed in professional learning communities. Each staff member, with collaborative consultant support, is responsible for plan completion, sharing with colleagues, and implementing as indicated. Specific partnering materials such as family communication tools, will be identified and shared. The *FSP Tiered Guide* will be consulted in developing action plans.
- In each grade, 95% of students will complete homework assignments on time during April, as measured by the school computerized class reporting program. Classroom teachers and collaborative consultants are responsible for student data entry, compilation, and goal completion.
- Of family members in all grades, 70% will attend at least one school event focusing on students by May 1, as measured by disaggregated participation data and event feedback. Event chairs and collaborative consultants are responsible for data collection and goal completion.
- Professional learning communities and leadership teams will include FSP and homework completion on their discussion agendas for every biweekly meeting all year, as marked in written notes. Community team facilitators, administrators, and collaborative consultants are responsible for data collection and goal completion.
- The RtI problem-solving and special education multidisciplinary teams will invite families and students (when appropriate) to participate as team members in all planning of assessments, interventions, or program placements during the year, as measured by family feedback and participation percentages. Respective team leaders and collaborative consultants are responsible for data collection and goal completion.

> **FSP TOOLS USED:** *Action Plan, Tiered Guide*

IMPLEMENT: Follow Plan as Intended; Monitor Progress

The foundation and each partnering tier include specific implementation details and data collection.

Foundation

The majority of school staff members embrace the idea of a "marketing campaign" focusing on student success as a shared responsibility, as do the active family members in the parent-teacher organization. This was after a presentation, discussion, and materials distribution about the FSP research and legal rationale, including the school data on multiple Fs and homework. A specific slogan is chosen, "Our Families and Staff Partner for Kids!," with the three foundational philosophical statements listed below the slogan (student success, shared responsibility, and unique expertise and cultures). A family-friendly communication explaining the school data and research is prepared, with family representatives helping to design the message. There is a banner for the school entrance.

> **FSP TOOLS USED:** *Legal and Research Rationale Stakeholder Slides, Wallet Reminder Cards*

Universal Tier

Each staff member completes a personal action plan identifying how he or she will invite families to share in responsibilities. Building relationships, creating welcoming settings, using two-way communication, and educating partners are all listed as key areas to address in practical planning. Departments and teams decide how to include FSP in regard to students into their regular meetings so that ideas can be shared and support offered to peers. A letter from the principal is sent to all families by mail and e-mail and is placed on the Web site. The letter explains the FSP focus of the school and the results of the survey data, sharing how families report wanting to support their students and to partner, but that there are challenges. Simple home scripts and actions for families are included, with a request for feedback. The Student Council is tapped, given information, and asked for their participation. The members help by deciding to "let students in on the deal"—that their families are being asked to work more closely with the teachers and work through the individual class representatives.

Specific homework success expectations for each class are shared with students, who are asked to discuss these with their families. Information on solving problems if they occur is shared with families and students. All families are asked to respond in writing, by e-mail, or by telephone message with their comments (two-way). Follow-up contact is made to those who do not respond in the traditional ways. Interactive homework assignments are provided so that families connect with the classroom learning. "Homework help" sessions for students and families with staff are from seven to eight each morning, five to seven most evenings, and on Saturdays; so they are available, staff receive compensatory time by coming in late or leaving early. Rides are carpooled if necessary. Also, afterschool volunteers provide supervision with a community "youth house" so that students can have structured time, computer access, and adult supervision. The parent-teacher organization decides to implement "outreach" invitations to all families and personally invite families who have not come to school according to office records.

FSP TOOLS USED: *Action Plan, Two-Way Homework, Principal Two-Way Welcome Letter/Newsletter, Teacher Two-Way Welcome Letter, Family Sharing Sheet, Event Feedback, Guest Response Card*

Targeted-Intensive Tiers

More personalized and focused partnering concerning homework completion is implemented for struggling students and families. Because there is schoolwide information sharing about the partnering efforts in regard to specific goals, families and teachers are openly communicating about identified students in many situations. There is a standard treatment protocol intervention for homework completion concerns, including required family and student education seminars and individual school-home-school notes. For a few students and families, individualized assessment and intervention are implemented as issues are often complex and multifaceted. Families and students team interventions with staff as full participants. RtI problem solving and multidisciplinary team leaders, with the help of the FSP collaborative consultants, invite and support family members, including students, as team members in planning student interventions.

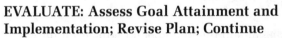

FSP TOOLS USED: *School-Home-School or Home-School-Home Note, Teaming Invitation, Team Family Information, Team Intervention Plan with Strengths and Family Coordination, Teaming Questions for Families and Educators to Ask Together, Teaming Interventions: What Families Need to Know, Permission for Diagnostic/ Prescriptive Assessment, Teaming Feedback, Sociocultural Educational Partnering Interview*

EVALUATE: Assess Goal Attainment and Implementation; Revise Plan; Continue

Data are collected monthly and shared with stakeholders as related to each of the major goals of the school. Charts are created by students and posted on the Web site and placed in the newsletter. Personal staff action plans are reviewed by individuals and sometimes with colleagues or administrators, depending on the situation. End-of-year data, related to specific goals, are as follows:

- FSP rationale will be shared with all staff, families, and students through presentations, Web site, written information, and CD availability.
  Result: 98% of families, staff, and students responded to having accessed the information; responses or feedback were by phone messages or in writing.

- Each school staff member will complete an individual action plan to include families in partnering for student school success, with a focus on engaged learning behavior, specifically homework completion. Each will use the *FSP Tiered Guide.*
  Result: 100% of staff, completed and reviewed individual FSP action plans; tools and materials were shared.

- In each grade, 95% of students will complete home-work assignments on time.
  Result: 80% of students in each grade completed homework assignments on time during April, an increase of 35%.

- Of family members, 70% will attend at least one school event focusing on students during the year.
  Result: 80% of family members attended at least one school event outside of back-to-school night and provided feedback that is being used to improve activities.

- Professional learning communities and leadership teams will include FSP and homework completion on their discussion agendas for every meeting.
  Result: 100% of meetings included FSP and homework sharing or discussion.

- The RtI problem-solving and special education multi-disciplinary teams will invite families and students to participate as team members in any planning of assessments, interventions, or program placements.
  Result: 100% of the time families were invited as team members; 89% of families and students participated either by ongoing two-way communication or by attending meetings and providing team feedback.

In revising and continuing FSP, the school mental health professionals and administrators are planning on continuing goals, forming family and student advisory committees, and developing a "family-to-family" component of their FSP headed by the parent-teacher organization. The FSP focus on student school success will be extended to include another aspect of engaged learning, school attendance, as data indicate 16% of students exhibit multiple monthly absences. Both family and staff data indicate commitment to continuing the FSP integration into everyday practices. Data also show that the collaborative consultant facilitation has supported question answering, discussion of personal and system hurdles, data collection, and partnering in finding workable solutions to time and logistical challenges.

OUR FINAL WORDS

As we end, we think of the inspiration we feel when others share their experiences with us as we work in the field. Using actual words from family members and educators can provide encouragement and humor to those implementing FSP. We have used some of these words to begin each of our chapters. Here are some of our other favorite quotations. We encourage readers to add their own words as they practice FSP.

- Aren't we already doing this? Isn't this just common sense? (A school board member after hearing about FSP plans at a school)

- Why haven't we done this before? It's great. My kids are already turning in more homework than last year. (A middle school teacher in talking about having recently contacted each of her students' families at the beginning of the school year)

- I didn't know I had permission to talk directly to parents. I thought I had to go to the counselor or dean first. The only exposure to working with parents I had in my teacher education was one four-hour seminar on "How to Survive Parent-Teacher Conferences." (A first-year high school foreign language teacher at an FSP training session)

- When I call myself a partner on my child's team, I no longer cry at meetings. We get much more accomplished, focus on progress, and I always leave with a "to do" list. (A parent of a child with a disability)

- I have never understood why my pediatrician always asks me detailed questions about how I see my child, and some of his teachers, at times, don't seem to want my information. And when he is ill, the pediatrician asks me to monitor his progress and communicate frequently with him, and when he is struggling with an issue at school, some of his teachers don't ask me about what I am seeing at home. (A parent of a child with a disability)

- All the parents want to know what is going on in the classroom. A teacher needs to think of creative ways to link them into what we are doing. Sending home links to podcasts, class Web sites, and weekly e-mail blogs are some easily accessed electronic tools—they are also fun for everyone. (A middle school language arts teacher)

- Do administrators know about this? (A teacher after an FSP class in which the research, legal, and reform rationale were shared)

- I never know what my role is as a parent in my third grader's education. I need someone to tell me what to do. Please. (A father who is chief executive officer of a large company)

- Everyone on our child's team seemed so surprised to know we had a tutor coming every week to work with our seventh grader in math (and had for a year), but then as the team members (including us!) thought about it, we realized that no one from school had ever asked, and we, the family, had never thought to share it with anyone at school. We all felt silly as we could have been aligning school and home efforts, making it much more productive for our student. (Parents of a struggling student in the RtI process)

- We made frequent home visits to our most truant students. It was worth every minute as now each comes regularly. Our families know we care about their students' success and that we aren't giving up on them. (Special education administrator)

- I am so glad we are discussing this now since my biggest professional fear is how to work well with families. It is just so important. (School psychology graduate student in FSP class)

- We can do this. We just have to talk about it and move some things around. I think it is the answer. I am a parent, and it just feels right. (A high school teacher talking to her team after attending an FSP training session)

References

Adams, D., Boyd, K., Cunningham, D., & Gailunas-Johnson, A. (2003). *Including every parent: A step-by-step guide to engage and empower parents at your school.* Chicago: Independent Publisher's Group.

Adams, K., & Christenson, S. L. (2000). Trust and the family-school relationship: Examination of parent-teacher differences in elementary and secondary grades. *Journal of School Psychology, 38,* 477–497.

Allen, J. (2007). *Creating welcoming schools: A practical guide to home-school partnerships with diverse families.* New York: Teachers College Press.

Amato, P. R., & Gilbreth, J. G. (1999). Nonresident fathers and children's well-being: A meta-analysis. *Journal of Marriage and the Family, 61,* 557–573.

American School Counseling Association. (2004). *Ethical standards for school counselors.* Alexandria, VA: Author.

Anderson, A. R., Christenson, S. L., & Lehr, C. A. (2004). School completion and student engagement: Information and strategies for educators. In A. S. Canter, L. Z. Paige, M. D. Roth, I. Romero, & S. A. Carroll (Eds.), *Helping children at home and at school II: Handouts for families and educators* (pp. S2-65–S2-68). Bethesda, MD: National Association of School Psychologists. Retrieved February 18, 2010, from http://ici.umn.edu/checkandconnect/publications/default.html#manual

Anderson, A. R., Christenson, S. L., Sinclair, M. F., & Lehr, C. A. (2004). Check & Connect: The importance of relationships for promoting engagement with school. *Journal of School Psychology, 42*(2), 95–113.

Astone, N., & McLanahan, S. (1991). Family structure, parental practices, and high school completion. *American Sociological Review, 56,* 309–320.

Baker, D., & Stevenson, D. (1986). Mothers' strategies for children's school achievement: Managing the transition to high school. *Sociology of Education, 59,* 156–166.

Bandura, A. (1977). *Social learning theory.* New York: General Learning Press.

Barnard, W. M. (2004). Parent involvement in elementary school and educational attainment. *Children and Youth Services Review, 26*, 39–62.

Bouffard, S., & Malone, H. (2007). *Complementary learning in action: Alignment Nashville.* Retrieved September 26, 2009, from http://www.hfrp.org/complementary-learning/publications-resources/complementary-learning-in-action-alignment-nashville

Bridgeland, J. M., Dilulio, J. J., Streeter, R. T., & Mason, J. R. (2008). *One dream, two realities: Perspectives of parents on America's high schools.* Washington, DC: Civic Enterprises. Retrieved April 8, 2009, from http://www.civicenterprises.net/pdfs/onedream.pdf

Brock, S. (2002). Crisis theory: A foundation for the comprehensive crisis prevention and intervention team. In S. Brock, P. Lazarus, & S. Jimerson (Eds.), *Best practices in school crisis prevention and intervention* (pp. 5–22). Bethesda, MD: National Association of School Psychologists.

Bronfenbrenner, U. (1979). *The ecology of human development.* Cambridge, MA: Harvard University Press.

Bronfenbrenner, U. (1986). Ecology of the family as a context for human development. Research perspectives. *Developmental Psychology, 22*, 723–742.

Brown-Chidsey, R. (2005). *Assessment for intervention: A problem-solving approach.* New York: Guilford.

Bryan, J. B, & Pelco, L. (2006). *School Psychologist Involvement in Partnerships Survey (SPIPS).* Williamsburg, VA: William and Mary School of Education.

Bryk, A. S., & Schneider, B. L. (2002). *Trust in schools: A core resource for improvement.* New York: Russell Sage Foundation.

Burns, M. K., & Gibbons, K. (2008). *Implementing response-to-intervention in elementary and secondary schools: Procedures to assure scientific-based procedures.* New York: Routledge.

Burns, M. K., Wiley, H. I., Viglietta, E. (2008). Best practices in implementing effective problem-solving teams. In A. Thomas & J. Grimes (Eds.), *Best practices in school psychology V* (pp. 1633–1644). Bethesda, MD: National Association of School Psychologists.

Callendar, W. (2007). The Idaho results-based model: Implementing response-to-intervention statewide. In S. R. Jimerson, M. K. Burns, & A. M. VanderHeyden (Eds.), *Handbook of response to intervention: The science and practice of assessment and intervention* (pp. 331–342). New York: Springer.

Chalfant, J. C., Pysh, M. V., & Moultrie, R. (1979). Teacher assistance teams: A model for within-building problem-solving. *Learning Disabilities Quarterly, 2,* 85–95.

Chapman, R. (2005). *The everyday guide to special education law. A handbook for parents, teachers, and other professionals.* Denver, CO: Legal Center for People With Disabilities and Older People.

Chavkin, N. F. (2003). Preparing educators for school-family partnerships. *The LSS Review, 2,* 1–3.

Cherry Creek Schools. (2006). *Response to intervention RtI/problem-solving process: Essentials.* Greenwood Village, CO: Author.

Christenson, S. L. (1995). Families and schools: What is the role of the school psychologist? *School Psychology Quarterly, 10,* 118–132.

Christenson, S. L. (2004). The family-school partnership: An opportunity to promote the learning competence of all students. *School Psychology Review, 33,* 83–104.

Christenson, S. L., & Anderson, A. (2002). The centrality of the learning context for students' academic enabler skills. *Journal of School Psychology, 31,* 378–393.

Christenson, S. L., & Carlson, C. (2005). Evidence-based parent and family interventions in school psychology: State of scientifically based practice. *School Psychology Quarterly, 20,* 525–528.

Christenson, S. L., & Godber, Y. (2001). Enhancing constructive family-school connections. In J. N. Hughes, A. M. La Greca, & J. C. Conoley (Eds.), *Handbook of psychological services for children and adolescents* (pp. 455–476). New York: Oxford University Press.

Christenson, S. L., Godber, Y., & Anderson, A. (2003). Critical issues facing families and educators. *The LSS Review, 2,* 8–9.

Christenson, S. L., Hurley, C. M., Sheridan, S. M., & Fenstermacher, K. (1997). Parents' and school psychologists' perspectives on parent involvement skills. *School Psychology Review, 26,* 111–130.

Christenson, S. L., & Reschly, A. (2010). *Handbook of school-family partnerships.* New York: Routledge.

Christenson, S. L., Reschly, A. L., Appleton, J. J., Berman-Young, S., Spanjers, D. M., & Varro, P. (2008). Best practices in fostering school engagement. In A. Thomas & J. Grimes (Eds.), *Best practices in school psychology V* (pp. 1099–1120). Bethesda, MD: National Association of School Psychologists.

Christenson, S. L., & Sheridan, S. M. (2001). *Schools and fami-lies: Creating essential connections for learning.* New York: Guilford.

Christenson, S. L., Thurlow, M. L., Sinclair, M. F., Kaibel, C. M., Reschly, A. L., Mavis, A., & Pohl, A. (2008). *Check & Connect: A comprehensive student engagement intervention manual.* Minneapolis, MN: Institute on Community Engagement.

Clark, R. M. (1990). Why disadvantaged students succeed: What hap-pens outside school is critical. *Public Welfare (Spring),* 17–23.

Clark, R. M. (2002, November). *In-school and out-of-school factors that build student achievement: Research-based implications for school instructional policy.* Naperville, IL: North Central Regional Educational Laboratory. Retrieved January 22, 2007, from http://www.ncrel.org/gap/clark/

Colorado Department of Education. (2008a). *Guidelines for identifying students with specific learning disabilities.* Retrieved March 20, 2009, from http://www.cde.state.co.us/cdesped/download/pdf/SLD_Guidelines.pdf

Colorado Department of Education. (2008b). *Response to inter-vention (RtI): A practitioner's guide to implementation.* Retrieved March 20, 2009, from http://www.cde.state.co.us/rti/ToolsResourcesRtI.htm

Colorado Department of Education. (2009). *Family and com-munity partnering: "On the team and at the table."* Retrieved June 28, 2009, from *http://www.cde.state.co.us/rti/FamilyCommunityToolkit.htm*

Connors, L. J., & Epstein, J. L. (1995). Parent and school part-nerships. In M. Bornstein (Ed.), *Handbook of parenting. Vol. 4, Applied and practical parenting* (pp. 437–458). Mahwah, NJ: Erlbaum.

Constantino, S. M. (2003). *Engaging all families: Creating a positive school culture by putting research into practice.* Lanham, MD: Scarecrow Education.

Constantino, S. M. (2008). *101 ways to create real family engage-ment.* Galax, VA: ENGAGE! Press.

Corey, M. S., & Corey, G. (2006). *Groups: Process and practice* (7th ed.). Belmont, CA: Thomson Brooks/Cole.

Cortiella, C. (2006). *NCLB and IDEA: What parents of students with disabilities need to know and do.* Minneapolis, MN: National Center on Educational Outcomes.

Curtis, M., Castillo, J. M., & Cohen, R. M. (2008). Best practices in system-level change. In A. Thomas & J. Grimes (Eds.), *Best practices in school psychology V* (pp. 887–902). Bethesda: MD: National Association of School Psychologists.

Dauber, S. L., & Epstein, J. L. (1993). Parents' attitudes and practices of involvement in inner-city elementary and middle schools. In N. E. Chavkin (Ed.), *Families and schools in a pluralistic society* (pp. 53–71). Albany: State University of New York Press.

Davies, D. (2001). Family participation in decision-making and advocacy. In D. Hiatt-Michael (Ed.), *Promising practices in family involvement in schools* (pp. 107–151). Greenwich, CT: Information Age.

Dawson, P. (2008). Best practices in managing homework. In A. Thomas & J. Grimes (Eds.), *Best practices in school psychology V* (pp. 969–982). Bethesda, MD: National Association of School Psychologists.

Dearing, E., Kreider, H., Simpkins, S., & Weiss, H. (2006). Family involvement in school and low-income children's literacy: Longitudinal associations between and within families. *Journal of Educational Psychology, 98,* 653–664.

de Carvalho, M. E. (2001). *Rethinking family-school relations: A critique of parent involvement in schooling.* London: Erlbaum.

Delgado-Gaitan, C. (1992). School matters in the Mexican-American home: Socializing children to education. *American Educational Research Journal, 29,* 495–513.

Delgado-Gaitan, C. (1994). *Consejos:* The power of cultural narrative. *Anthropology Education Quarterly, 25,* 298–316.

Delgado Gaitan, C. (2004). *Involving Latino families in schools.* Thousand Oaks, CA: Corwin Press.

Diamond, J. B., Wang, L., & Gomez, K. W. (2004). *African-American and Chinese-American parent involvement: The importance of race, class, and culture.* Research Digest. FINE Network. Retrieved December 6, 2009, from www.hfrp.org/publications-resources/publications-series/f amily-involvement-research-digests/african-american-and-chinese-american-parent-involvement-the-importance-of-r ace-class-and-culture

Duchnowski, A. J., & Kutash, K. (2007). *Family-driven care.* Tampa, FL: University of South Florida, Louis de la Parte Florida Mental Health Institute, Department of Child and Family Studies.

Dunst, C. J. (2002). Family-centered practices: Birth through high school. *Journal of Special Education, 36,* 139–147.

Dunst, C. J., & Trivette, C. M. (1987). Enabling and empowering families: Conceptual and intervention issues. *School Phychology Review, 16*(4), 443–456.

Dunst, C. J., Trivette, C. M., & Deal, A. G. (1994). *Supporting and strengthening families: Methods, strategies, and practices.* Cambridge, MA: Brookline Books.

Dunst, C. J., Trivette, C. M., & Deal, A. G. (2003). *Enabling and empowering families: Principles and guidelines for practice.* Newton, MA: Brookline Books.

Dupaul, G. J., Stoner, G., & O'Reilly, M. J. (2008). Best practices in classroom interventions for attention problems. In A. Thomas & J. Grimes (Eds.), *Best practices in school psychology V* (pp. 1421–1438). Bethesda: MD: National Association of School Psychologists.

Eagle, J. W., Dowd-Eagle, S. E., & Sheridan, S. M. (2008). Best practices in school-community partnering. In A. Thomas & J. Grimes (Eds.), *Best practices in school psychology V* (pp. 953–968). Bethesda, MD: National Association of School Psychologists.

Eber, L. (2003). *The art and science of wraparound.* Bloomington, IN: Forum on Education, Indiana University.

Eber, L., Rolf, K., & Schreiber, M. P. (1996). *A look at the 5-year ISBE EBD initiative: End of the year report for 1995–96.* LaGrange, IL: LaGrange Area of Special Education.

Eber, L., Sugai, G., Smith, C. R., & Scott, T. M. (2002). Wraparound and positive behavioral interventions and supports in schools. *Journal of Emotional and Behavioral Disorders, 10,* 171–180.

Ellis, D., & Hughes, K. (2002). *Partnerships by design: Cultivating effective and meaningful school-family-community partnerships.* Portland, OR: Northwest Regional Educational Laboratories.

Enyeart, C., Diehl, J., Hampden-Thompson, G., & Scotchmer, M. (2006). *School and parent interaction by household language and poverty status: 2002–03.* Washington, DC: Government Printing Office.

Epstein, J. L. (1995). School, family, and community partnerships: Caring for the children we share. *Phi Delta Kappan, 76,* 701–712.

Epstein, J. L. (2001). *School, family, and community partnerships: Preparing educators and improving schools.* Boulder, CO: Westview.

Epstein, J. L., & Becker, H. J. (1982). Teacher reported practices of parent involvement: Problems and possibilities. *Elementary School Journal, 88,* 108–118.

Epstein, J. L., Coates, L., Salinas, K. C., Sanders, M. G., & Simon, B. S. (1997). *School, family and community partnerships: Your handbook for action.* Thousand Oaks, CA: Corwin Press.

Epstein, J. L., & Sanders, M. G. (2002). Family, school, and community partnerships. In M. H. Bornstein (Ed.), *Handbook of parenting* (2nd ed., Vol. 5, pp. 407–437). Mahwah, NJ: Erlbaum.

Epstein, J. L., Sanders, M. G., Simon, B. S., Salinas, K. C., Jansorn, N. R., & Van Voorhis, F. L. (2002). *School family and community partnerships: Your handbook for action* (2nd ed.). Thousand Oaks, CA: Corwin Press.

Epstein, J. L., Simon, B. S., & Salinas, K. C. (1997). Involving parents in homework in the middle grades. *Phi Delta Kappan Research Bulletin, 18,* 1–4.

Ervin, R. A., & Schaughency, E. (2008). Best practices in accessing the systems change literature. In A. Thomas & J. Grimes (Eds.), *Best practices in school psychology V* (pp. 853–874). Bethesda: MD: National Association of School Psychologists.

Esler, A. N., Godber, Y., & Christenson, S. (2008). Best practices in supporting home-school collaboration. In A. Thomas & J. Grimes (Eds.), *Best practices in school psychology V* (pp. 917–936). Bethesda, MD: National Association of School Psychologists.

Fadiman, A. (1997). *The spirit catches you and you fall down: A Hmong child, her American doctors, and the collision of two cultures.* New York, NY: Farrar, Straus, and Giroux.

Fagan, J., & Palm, G. (2003). *Fathers and early childhood programs.* Clifton Park, NY: Thomson Delmar Learning.

Fantuzzo, J., Tighe, E., & Childs, S. (2000). Family involvement questionnaire: A multivariate assessment of family participation in early childhood education. *Journal of Educational Psychology, 92,* 367–376.

Fege, A. F. (2008). Family involvement policy: Past, present, and future. *The Evaluation Exchange. 14* (1&2), 16–17. Retrieved February 1, 2001, from http://www.hfrp.org/evaluation/the-evaluation-exchange/issue-archive/current-issue-building-the-future-of-family-involvement/family-involvement-policy-past-present-and-future

Fishel, M. & Ramirez, L. (2005). Evidence-based parent involvement interventions with school-aged children. *School Psychology Quarterly, 20,* 371–402.

Fixsen, D. L., Naoom, S. F., Blasé, K. A., Friedman, R. M., & Wallace, F. (2005). *Implementation research: A synthesis of the literature.* Retrieved July 10, 2009, from http://nirn. fmhi.usf.edu/resources/publications/Monograph/pdf/ Mongraph_full.pdf

Flouri, E. (2005). *Fathering and child outcomes.* West Sussex, England: Wiley.

Friedberg, R. D., & McClure, J. M. (2002). *Clinical practice of cognitive therapy with children and adolescents.* New York: Guilford Press.

Future of School Psychology Task Force on Family-School Partnerships. (2007). *Family-school partnership training modules.* Retrieved March 31, 2009, from http://fsp.unl. edu/future_index.html

Gallimore, R., & Goldenberg, C. (2001). Analyzing cultural models and settings to connect minority achievement and school improvement research. *Educational Psychologist, 36,* 45–56.

Garcia Coll, C., & Chatman, C. (2005). Ethnic and racial diversity. In H. Weiss, H. Kreider, M. E. Lopez, & C. Chatman (Eds.), *Preparing educators to involve families: From theory to practice* (pp. 135–142). London: Sage.

Gee, J. P. (2004). *Situated language and learning: A critique of traditional schooling.* New York: Routledge.

Gill, B. P. & Schlossman, S. L. (2003). Parents and the politics of homework: Some historical perspectives. *Teachers College Record, 105,* 846–871.

Gilman, R., & Chard, K. M. (2007). Cognitive-behavioral and behavioral approaches. In H. T. Prout & D. T. Brown (Eds.), *Counseling and psychotherapy with children and adolescents* (pp. 241–278). Hoboken, NJ: Wiley.

Gladwell, M. (2002). *The tipping point.* New York: Little, Brown.

González, N., & Moll, L. (2002). Cruzando el puente: Building bridges to funds of knowledge. *Educational Policy, 16,* 623–641.

Graden, J. L., Stollar, S. A., & Poth, R. L. (2007). The Ohio integrated systems model: Overview and lessons learned. In S. R. Jimerson, M. K. Burns, & A. M. VanderHeyden (Eds.), *Handbook of response to intervention: The science and practice of assessment and intervention* (pp. 288–299). New York: Springer.

Greenberg, M. T., Weissberg, R. P., O'Brien, M. U., Zins, J. E., Fredericks, L., Resnik, H., & Elias, M. J. (2003). Enhancing school-based prevention and youth development through coordinated social, emotional, and academic learning. *American Psychologist, 58,* 466–474.

Grolnick, W. S., Ryan, R. M., & Deci, E. L. (1991). Inner resources for school achievement: Motivational mediators of children's perceptions of their parents. *Journal of Educational Psychology, 83,* 508–517.

Grolnick, W. S., & Slowiaczek, M. L. (1994). Parent involvement in children's schooling: A multidimensional conceptualization and motivational model. *Child Development, 64,* 237–252.

Gunn, W. B., Haley, J., & Lyness, A. M. (2007). Systemic approaches: Family therapy. In H. T. Prout & D. T. Brown (Eds.), *Counseling and psychotherapy with children and adolescents* (pp. 388–417). Hoboken, NJ: Wiley.

Harris, M. B., Franklin, C., & Hopson, L. (2007). The design of social work services. In P. Meares (Ed.), *Social work services in schools* (pp. 293–3160). New York: Pearson Education.

Harry, B. (1992). *Cultural diversity, families, and the special education system: Communication and empowerment.* New York: Teachers College Press.

Henderson, A. T. (2001). *The evidence continues to grow.* Washington, DC: Center for Law and Education.

Henderson, A. T., & Berla, N. (1994). *A new generation of evidence: The family is critical for student achievement.* Washington, DC: Center for Law and Education.

Henderson, A. T., & Mapp, K. L. (2002). *A new wave of evidence: The impact of school, family, and community connections on achievement.* Austin, TX: National Center for Family and Community Connections With Schools.

Henderson, A. T., Mapp, K. L., Johnson, V. R., & Davies, D. (2007). *Beyond the bake sale: The essential guide to family-school partnerships.* New York: New Press.

Herr, C. M., & Bateman, B. D. (2006). *Writing measurable IEP goals and objectives.* Verona, WI: Attainment.

Hess, R., Holloway, S., Dickson, W., & Price, G. (1984). Maternal variables as predictors of children's school readiness and later achievement in vocabulary and mathematics in sixth grade. *Child Development, 55,* 1902–1912.

Hicks, D. (2002). *Reading lives: Working-class children and literacy learning.* New York: Teachers College Press.

Hill, N. E. (2001). Parenting and academic socialization as they relate to school readiness: The roles of ethnicity and family income. *Journal of Educational Psychology, 93,* 686–697.

Hill, N. E., Castellino, D. R., Lansford, J. E., Nowlin, P., Dodge, K. A., Bates, J. E., & Petit, J. S. (2004). Parent academic involvement as related to school behavior, achievement, and aspirations: Demographic variations across adolescence. *Child Development, 75,* 1491–1509.

Holloway, S. D., Fuller, B., Ramaud, M. F., & Eggers-Piérola, C. (1997). *Through my own eyes: Single mothers and the cultures of poverty.* Cambridge, MA: Harvard University Press.

Hoover-Dempsey, K. V., & Sandler, H. (1995). Parental involvement in children's education: Why does it make a difference? *Teachers College Record, 97,* 310–331.

Hoover-Dempsey, K., & Sandler, H. (1997). Why do parents become involved in their children's education? *Review of Educational Research, 67,* 3–42.

Hoover-Dempsey, K. V., Walker, J. M. T., Sandler, H., Whetsel, D., Green, C. L., Wilkins, A. L., & Closson, K. E. (2005). Why do parents become involved? Research findings and implications. *The Elementary School Journal, 106*(2), 105–130.

Individuals with Disabilities Education Improvement Act of 2004, PL 108–446, 118 Stat. 2647 (2004).

Izzo, C. V., Weissberg, R. P., Kasprow, W. J., & Fendrich, M. (1999). Longitudinal assessment of teacher perceptions of parent involvement in children's education and school performance. *American Journal of Community Psychology, 27,* 817–839.

Jenkins, T. (2007). *When a child struggles in school.* Charleston, SC: Advantage.

Jennings, D. (2008). *RtI implementation planning tool.* Retrieved April 8, 2009, from http://www.tacommunities. org/document/list/p/folder_5071%252Ffolder_5073%25 2Ffolder_5162

Jeynes, W. H. (2005). *Parental involvement and student achievement: A meta-analysis.* Harvard Family Research Project. Retrieved January 1, 2007, from http://www.gse.harvard. edu/hfrp/publications_resources/publications_series/ family_involvement_research_digests/parental_involvement_and_student_achievement_a_meta_analysis

Jeynes, W. H. (2007). The relationship between parental involvement and urban secondary school student achievement: A meta-analysis. *Urban Education, 42,* 82–110.

Jimerson, S. R., Reschly, A. L., & Hess, R. S. (2008). Best practices in increasing the likelihood of school completion. In A. Thomas & J. Grimes (Eds.), *Best practices in school psychology V* (pp. 2–26). Bethesda, MD: National Association of School Psychologists.

Johns, K. J., Patrick, J. A., & Rutherford, K. J. (2008). Best practices in district-wide positive behavior supports. In A. Thomas & J. Grimes (Eds.), *Best practices in school psychology V* (pp. 721–734). Bethesda, MD: National Association of School Psychologists.

Jones, J. M. (2009). *The psychology of multiculturalism in the schools: A primer for practice, training, and research.* Bethesda, MD: National Association of School Psychologists.

Jordan, G. E., Snow, C. E., & Porche, M. V. (2000). Project EASE: The effect of a family literacy project on kindergarten students' early literacy skills. *Reading Research Quarterly, 35,* 524–546.

Jurbergs, S., Palcic, J., & Kelly, M. L. (2007). School-home notes with and without response cost: Increasing attention and academic performance in low-income children with attention-deficit hyperactivity disorder. *School Psychology Quarterly, 22,* 358–379.

Kampwirth, T. J. (2006). *Collaborative consultation in the schools: Effective practices for students with learning and behavior problems* (3rd ed.). Upper Saddle River, NJ: Pearson Education.

Kelly, M. L. (1990). *School-home notes: Promoting children's classroom success.* New York: Guilford Press.

Kentucky Department of Education. (2007). *The missing part of the proficiency puzzle.* Frankfort, KY: Author. Retrieved March 20, 2009, from http://www.education.ky.gov/KDE/Instructional+Resources/Student+and+Family+Support/Parents+and+Families/The+Missing+Piece+of+the+Proficiency+Puzzle.htm

Klassen-Endrizzi, C. (2004). We've got to talk: Redefining our work with families. *Language Arts, 81,* 323–333.

Knoff, H. (2008). Best practices in implementing statewide positive behavioral support systems. In A. Thomas & J. Grimes (Eds.), *Best practices in school psychology V* (pp. 903–916). Bethesda, MD: National Association of School Psychologists.

Kovaleski, J. F., Gickling, E. E., Morrow, H., & Swank, P. (1999). High versus low implementation of instructional support teams: A case for maintaining program fidelity. *Remedial and Special Education, 20,* 170–183.

Kubler-Ross, E. (1969). *On death and dying.* New York: Collier.

Lareau, A. (2003). *Unequal childhoods: Class, race, and family life.* Berkley: University of California Press.

Larson, J. (2005). *Think first: Addressing aggressive behavior in secondary schools.* New York: Guilford Press.

Laugeson, E. A., Frankel, F., Mogil, C., & Dillon, A. R. (2009). Parent-assisted social skills training to improve friendships in teens with autism spectrum disorders. *Journal of Autism and Developmental Disorders, 23,* 596–606.

Lawrence-Lightfoot, S. (2002). *The essential conversation: What parents and teachers can learn from each other.* New York: Ballantine Books.

Leuder, D. C. (2000). *Creating partnerships with parents: An educator's guide.* Lanham, MA: Scarecrow Press.

Little, P. (2009). *Supporting student outcomes through expanded learning opportunities.* Retrieved February 2, 2010, from http://www.hfrp.org/publications-resources/browse-our-publications/supporting-student-outcomes-through-expanded-learning-opportunities

Mantzicopoulos, P. Y. (2003). Flunking kindergarten after Head Start: An inquiry into the contribution of individual contextual variables. *Journal of Educational Psychology, 95,* 268–278.

Manz, P. H., Fantuzzo, J. W., & Power, T. J. (2004). Multidimensional assessment of family involvement among urban elementary students. *Journal of School Psychology, 42,* 461–475.

Manz, P. J., Mautone, J. A., & Martin, S. D. (2009). School psychologists' collaborations with families: An exploratory study of the interrelationships of their perceptions of professional efficacy and school climate and demographic and training variables. *Journal of Applied School Psychology, 25,* 47–50.

Mapp, K. L. (2003). Having their say: Parents describe why and how they are engaged in their children's education. *School Community Journal, 13*(1), 35–64.

Marzano, R. J. (2003). *What works in schools: Translating research into action.* Alexandria, VA: Association for Supervision and Curriculum Development.

Mattingly, D. J., Prislin, R., McKenzie, T. L., Rodriguez, J. L., & Kayzar, B. (2002). Evaluating evaluations: The case of parent involvement programs. *Review of Education Research, 72,* 549–576.

McBride, B. A., Schoppe-Sullivan, S. J., & Ho, M. H. (2005). The mediating role of fathers' school involvement on student achievement. *Journal of Applied Developmental Psychology, 26,* 201–216.

McConaughy, S., Kay, P., Welkowitz, J., Hewitt, K., & Fitzgerald, M. (2008). *Collaborating with parents for early school success: The achieving-behaving-caring program.* New York: Guilford Press.

McConaughy, S. H., Kay, P., & Fitzgerald, M. (1999). The achieving-behaving-caring project for preventing ED: Two-year outcomes. *Journal of Emotional and Behavioral Disorders, 7*(4), 224–239.

McNiff., J., & Whitehead, J. (2005). *All you need to know about action research.* London: Sage.

McWayne, C., Hampton, V., Fantuzzo, J., Cohen, H. L., & Sekino, Y. (2004). A multivariate examination of parent involvement and the social and academic competencies of urban kindergarten children. *Psychology in Schools, 41,* 363–377.

Merriam-Webster. (2004). *Merriam Webster's collegiate dictionary.* Springfield, MA: Merriam-Webster.

Miedel, W. T., & Reynolds, A. J. (1999). Parent involvement in early intervention for disadvantaged children: Does it matter? *Journal of School Psychology, 37,* 379–402.

Miller, D., & Kraft, N. (2008). Best practices in communicating with and involving parents. In A. Thomas & J. Grimes (Eds.), *Best practices in school psychology V* (pp. 937–951). Bethesda, MD: National Association of School Psychologists.

Miller, G. E., & Choy, A. (2009, November). *Enhancing family engagement through coffee connects.* Poster presented at the annual meeting of the Colorado Society of School Psychology, Vail, CO.

Minke, K. (2008). Parent-teacher relationships. In B. Bear & K. Minke (Eds.), *Children's needs III: Development, prevention, and intervention* (pp. 73–86). Bethesda, MD: National Association of School Psychologists.

Minke, K. M., & Anderson, K. J. (2008). Best practices in facilitating family-school meetings. In A. Thomas & J. Grimes (Eds.), *Best practices in school psychology V* (pp. 969–982). Bethesda: MD: National Association of School Psychologists.

Moses, K. (1983). The impact of initial diagnosis: Mobilizing family resources. In J. Mulick & S. Pueschel (Eds.), *Parent-professional partnerships in developmental disability services* (pp. 1–16). Cambridge, MA: American Guild.

Naseef, R. A. (2001). *Special children, challenged parents: The struggles and rewards of raising a child with a disability.* Baltimore, MD: Brooks.

National Association of School Psychologists. (2000). *Principles for professional ethics: Guidelines for the provision of school psychological services.* Bethesda, MD: Author.

National Association of School Psychologists. (2005). *Home-school collaboration: Establishing partnerships to enhance educational outcomes* [Position statement]. Bethesda, MD: Author.

National Association of Social Workers. (1999). *NASW code of ethics.* Washington, DC: Author.

National Association of Social Workers. (2002). *NASW standards for school social work services.* Washington, DC: Author.

National Association of State Directors of Special Education. (2006). *Response to intervention: Policy considerations and implementation.* Alexandria, VA: Author.

National Family, School, and Community Engagement Working Group. (2009). *Recommendations for federal policy.* Retrieved February 2, 2010, from http://www.hfrp.org/publications-resources/browse-our-publications/national-family-school-and-community-engagement-working-group-recommendations-for-federal-policy

National Parent Teachers Association. (1998). Reaching out to others: Overcoming barriers to parent/family involvement. Retrieved July 22, 2009, from http://www.pta.org/programs/education/barriers.htm

National Parent Teachers Association. (2000). *Building successful partnerships: A guide for developing parent and family involvement programs.* Bloomington, IN: National Educational Services.

National Parent Teachers Association. (2009). PTA national standards for family-school partnerships: An implementation guide. Retrieved December 6, 2009, from http://www.pta.org/Documents/National_Standards_Implementation_Guide_2009.pdf

NCLB Action Briefs. (2004). *Parent involvement.* Public Education Network and National Coalition for Parent Involvement in Education. Retrieved October 29, 2009, from http://www. ncpie.org/nclbaction/parent_involvement.html

Nevin, A. I. (2008). Why are parent partnerships a puzzlement? A commentary. *Journal of Educational and Psychological Consultation, 18,* 259–263.

No Child Left Behind Act of 2001. PL 107–110. 115 Stat. 1452 (2002).

Ortiz, S. O., Flanagan, D. P., & Dynda, A. M. (2008). Best practices in working with culturally diverse children and families. In A. Thomas & J. Grimes (Eds.), *Best practices in school psychology V* (pp. 1721–1738). Bethesda, MD: National Association of School Psychologists.

Patrikakou, E. N., & Weissberg, R. P. (2000). Parents' perceptions of teacher outreach and parent involvement in children's education. *Journal of Prevention and Intervention in the Community, 20*(1–2), 103–119.

Patrikakou, E. N., Weissberg, R. P., Manning, J. B., & Walberg, H. J. (2003). School-family partnerships: Promoting the social, emotional, and academic growth of children. *The LSS Review, 2,* 1–3.

Patrikakaou, E. N., Weissberg, R. P., Redding, S., & Walberg, H. J. (Eds.). (2005). *School-family partnerships for children's learning.* New York: Teachers College Press.

Peacock, G. G., & Collett, B. R. (2010). *Collaborative home/school interventions: Evidence-based solutions for emotional, behavioral, and academic problems.* New York: Guilford.

Peterson, D. W., Prasse, D. P., Shinn, M. R., & Swerdlik, M. E. (2007). The Illinois flexible service delivery model: A problem-solving model initiative. In S. R. Jimerson, M. K. Burns, & A. M. VanderHeyden (Eds.), *Handbook of response to intervention: The science and practice of assessment and intervention* (pp. 300–318). New York: Springer.

Pianta, R., & Walsh, D. B. (1996). *High-risk children in schools: Constructing sustaining relationships.* New York: Routledge.

Pleck, J. H., & Masciadrelli, B. P. (2004). Paternal involvement by U.S. resident fathers: Levels, sources, and consequences. In M. E. Lamb (Ed.), *The role of the father in child development* (4th ed., pp. 222–271). New York: Wiley.

Pomerantz, E. M., Grolnick, W. S., & Price, C. E. (2005). The role of parents in how children approach school: A dynamic perspective. In A. J. Elliot & C. S. Dweck (Eds.), *The handbook of competence and motivation* (pp. 259–278). New York: Guilford Press.

Powell, D. R. (1993). Supporting parent-child relationships in the early years: Lessons learned and yet to be learned. In T. H. Brubaker (Ed.), *Family relations: Challenges for the future* (pp. 79–97). Newbury Park, CA: Sage.

President's Commission on Excellence in Special Education. (2002). *A new era: Revitalizing special education for children and their families.* Washington, DC: U.S. Department of Education, Office of Special Education and Rehabilitative Services.

Prout, H. T., & Brown, D. T. (2007). *Counseling and psychotherapy with children and adolescents: Theory and practice for school and clinical settings* (4th ed.). Hoboken, NJ: Wiley.

Raines, J. C. (2008). *Evidence-based practice in school mental health.* New York: Oxford University Press.

Reschly, A., Coolong-Chaffin, M. A., Christenson, S. L., & Gutkin, T. (2007). Contextual influences and response to intervention: Critical issues and strategies. In S. R. Jimerson, M. K. Burns, & A. M. VanderHeyden (Eds.),(pp. 148–160). *Handbook of response to intervention: The science and practice of assessment and intervention.* New York: Springer.

Reyes, P., Scribner, J. D., & Scribner, A. P. (Eds.). (1999). *Lessons from high-performing Hispanic schools: Creating learning communities.* New York: Teachers College Press.

Rosenfield, S. (2008). *Best practices in instructional consultation and instructional consultation teams.* In A. Thomas & J. Grimes (Eds.), *Best practices in school psychology V* (pp. 1645–1660). Bethesda, MD: National Association of School Psychologists.

Rothman, R. (Ed.) *City Schools: How districts and communities can create smart education systems.* Cambridge, MA: Harvard Education Press.

Salinas, K., & Jansorn, N. (2004). *Promising partnership practices.* Baltimore, MD: Johns Hopkins University Center on School, Family and Community Partnerships.

Schmoker, M. (2006). *Results now: How we can achieve unprecedented improvements in teaching and learning.* Alexandria, VA: Association for Supervision and Curriculum Development.

Scott-Jones, D. (1995). Parent-child interactions and school achievement. In B. A. Ryan, G. R. Adams, T. P. Gullotta, R. P. Weissberg, & R. L. Hampton (Eds.), *The family-school connection: Theory, research, and practice* (pp. 75–107). Thousand Oaks, CA: Sage.

Seginer, R. (2006). Parents' educational involvement: A developmental ecology perspective. *Parenting: Science and Practice, 6,* 1–48.

Sénéchal, M., & LeFevre, J. (2002). Parental involvement in the development of children's reading skill: A five-year longitudinal study. *Child Development, 73,* 445–460.

Sheldon, S. (2006). Improving student attendance with school, family, and community partnerships. *The Journal of Educational Research, 100,* 267–275.

Sheridan, S. M. (1997). Conceptual and empirical bases of conjoint behavioral consultation. *School Psychology Quarterly, 12,* 119–133.

Sheridan, S. M., & Kratochwill, T. R. (1992). Behavioral parent-teacher consultation: Conceptual and research considerations. *Journal of School Psychology, 29,* 117–139.

Sheridan, S. M., & Kratochwill, T. R. (2008). *Conjoint behavioral consultation: Promoting family-school connections and interventions.* New York: Springer.

Sheridan, S. M., & McCurdy, M. (2005). Ecological variables in school-based assessment and intervention planning. In R. Brown-Chidsey (Ed.), *Assessment for intervention: A problem-solving approach* (pp. 43–64). New York: Guilford.

Sheridan, S. M., Taylor, A., & Woods, K. (2008). Best practices for working with families: Instilling a family-centered approach. In A. Thomas & J. Grimes (Eds.), *Best practices in school psychology V* (pp. 995–1008). Bethesda, MD: National Association of School Psychologists.

Simon, B. S. (2001). Family involvement in high school: Predictors and effects. *NASSP Bulletin, 85*(627), 8–19.

Simon, B., & Epstein, J. L. (2001). School, family, and community partnerships: Linking theory to practice. In D. B. Haitt-Michael (Ed.), *Promising practices for family involvement in schools* (pp. 1–38). Greenwich, CT: Information Age.

Sinclair, M. F., Christenson, S. L., & Thurlow, M. L. (2005). Promoting school completion of urban secondary youth with emotional or behavioral disabilities. *Exceptional Children, 71,* 465–482.

Stanton-Salazar, R. (2001). *Manufacturing hope and despair: The school and kin support networks of U.S.-Mexican youth.* New York: Teachers College Press, pp. 1–106.

Stevens, B. A., & Tollafield, A. (2003). Creating comfortable and productive parent/teacher conferences. *Phi Delta Kappan, 84,* 521–524.

Stollar, S. A., Schaeffer, K. R., Skelton, S. M., Stine, K. C., Lateer-Huhn, A., & Poth, R. L. (2008). Best practices in professional development: An integrated, three-tier model of academic and behavior supports. In A. Thomas & J. Grimes (Eds.), *Best practices in school psychology V* (pp. 875–886). Bethesda, MD: National Association of School Psychologists.

Sue, D. W., & Sue, D. (2003). *Counseling the culturally diverse.* New York: Wiley.

Sugai, G., Horner, R. H., Sailor, W., Dunlap, G., Eber, L., Lewis, T., et al. (2005). *School-wide positive behavior support: Implementer's blueprint and self-assessment.* Eugene, OR: University of Oregon. Retrieved Febuary 21, 2010, from http://www.pbis.org/pbis_resource_detail_page.aspx?Type=3&PBIS_ResourceID=216

Teachman, J., & Paasch, K. (1998). The family and educational aspirations. *Journal of Marriage and the Family, 60,* 704–714.

Thomas, A., & Grimes, J. (2008). *Best practices in school psychology V.* Bethesda, MD: National Association of School Psychologists.

U.S. Bureau of the Census. (2004). Population predictions. Retrieved May 17, 2008, from http://www.census.gov/ipc/www/usinterimproj/

U.S. Department of Education. (2006). 34 CFR Part 300: Assistance to states for the education of children with disabilities and preschool grants for children with disabilities. Final rule. *Federal Register, 71,* 46783–46793.

U.S. Department of Education, Office of the Secretary, Office of Public Affairs. (2003). *No child left behind: A parents guide.* Washington, DC: Author.

Vaden-Kiernan, N., & McManus, J. (2005). *Parent and family involvement in education: 2002–03* (NCES 2005–043). U.S. Department of Education, National Center for Education Statistics. Washington, DC: U.S. Government Printing Office.

Valdés, G. (1996). *Con respeto: Bridging the distances between culturally diverse families and schools.* Sociology of Education Series, No. 9. New York: Teachers College Press.

Valenzuela, A. (1999). *Subtractive schooling: U.S. Mexican youth and the politics of caring.* New York: State University of New York Press.

Van Velsor, P., & Orozco, G. L. (2007). Involving low-income parents in the schools: Community-centric strategies for school counselors. *Professional School Counseling, 11,* 1–11.

Walker, J. M., Hoover-Dempsey, K. V., Whetsel, D. R., & Green, C. L. (2004). *Parental involvement in homework: A review of current research and its implications for teachers, after school program staff, and parent leaders.* Cambridge, MA: Harvard Family Research Project.

Webster-Stratton, C., & Reid, M. J. (2003). The incredible years parents, teachers and children's training series: A multifaceted treatment approach for young children with conduct problems. In A. E. Kazdin & J. R. Weisz (Eds.), *Evidence-based psychotherapies for children and adolescents* (pp. 224–238). New York: Guilford.

Webster-Stratton, C., Reid, M. J., & Hammond, M. (2001). Preventing conduct problems, promoting social competence: A parent and teacher training partnership in Head Start. *Journal of Clinical Child Psychology, 30,* 283–302.

Weiss, H., Caspe, M., & Lopez, M. E. (2006). *Family involvement in early childhood education.* Research Brief: Family Involvement Makes a Difference, 1. Boston: Harvard Family Research Project.

Weiss, H. B., Kreider, H., Lopez, M. E., & Chatman, C. M. (2005). *Preparing educators to involve families: From theory to practice.* Thousand Oaks, CA: Sage.

Weiss, H. B., & Stephen, N. (2010). From periphery to center: A new vision for family, school, and community partnerships. In S. Christenson & A. Reschly (Eds.), *Handbook of school-family partnerships* (pp. 448–472). New York: Routledge.

Wellman, B., & Lipton, L. (2004). *Data-driven dialogue: A facilitator's guide to collaborative inquiry.* Sherman, CT: MiraVia.

White, C. L. (2009). "What he wanted was real stories, but no one would listen": A child's literacy, a mother's understandings. *Language Arts, 86,* 431–439.

Wilson, C., & Dunst, C. J. (2002). Checking out family-centered help giving practices. *Young Exceptional Children, Monograph Series, 5,* 13–26.

Wright, J. (2007). *RtI toolkit: A practical guide for schools.* Port Chester, NY: Dude.

Wright, P. W. D., & Wright, P. D. (2005). *IDEA 2004.* Hartfield, VA: Harbor House Law Press.

Yell, M. L., & Stecker, P. M. (2003). Developing legally correct and educationally meaningful IEPs using curriculum-based measurement. *Assessment of Effective Instruction, 28*(3–4), 73–88.

Ysseldyke, J. E., & Christenson, S. L. (2002). *Functional assessment of academic behavior: Creating successful learning environments.* Longmont, CO: Sopris West.

Zhang, D., Miller, G. E., Ani, L., & Chen, H. F. (2009). *Assessing parent involvement: A content analysis of current measures.* In Press.

Zins, J. E., Weissberg, R. P., Wang, M. C., & Walberg, H. J. (Eds.). (2004). *Building academic success on social and emotional learning: What does the research say?* New York: Teachers College Press.

Index

CD Contents